CONTEMPORARY LAW SERIES

GEOFFREY C. HAZARD, Jr.

MICHELE TARUFFO

American Civil Procedure

An Introduction

[signature]

1997

Yale University Press   New Haven and London

Published with assistance from the foundation established in memory of Henry
Weldon Barnes of the Class of 1882, Yale College.

Set in Sabon Roman type by DEKR Corporation, Woburn, Massachusetts.
Printed in the United States of America by Vail-Ballou Press, Binghamton,
New York.

Library of Congress Cataloging-in-Publication Data

Hazard, Geoffrey C.
    American civil procedure : an introduction / Geoffrey C. Hazard,
Michele Taruffo.
        p.   cm. — (Contemporary law series)
    Includes bibliographical references and index.
    ISBN 0–300–05426–2
    1. Civil procedure—United States.   I. Taruffo, Michele.
II. Title.   III. Series.
KF8840.H27   1993
347.73'5—dc20
[347.3075]   93–4388

A catalogue record for this book is available from the British Library.

The paper in this book meets the guidelines for permanence and durability of the
Committee on Production Guidelines for Book Longevity of the Council on
Library Resources.

10 9 8 7 6 5 4 3 2 1

CONTENTS

The American legal system is a subject of general interest and importance. The United States is the leading industrial country in the world and one of the world's largest political democracies. The American political system has a distinctly legal character and the judiciary plays an especially important role in making public policy and defining private relationships. Civil litigation in the ordinary courts of justice is the principal mechanism through which this role is performed. Alexis de Tocqueville, the great nineteenth-century French observer of the American scene, noted that "there is hardly a political question in the United States which does not sooner or later turn into a judicial one."[1] Thus, such vital questions as equal treatment of racial minorities, legal limitations on the availability of abortion, and relationships between church and state are to an important extent governed by law pronounced by the courts rather than by the legislature. This book is designed to explain the procedure by which the courts resolve these questions to people interested in society and government.

The judicial system's importance in the American political system is well known. Most Americans recognize, for example, the name of the leading case concerning racial desegregation as *Brown v. Board of Education,* decided by the United States Supreme Court in 1954.[2] As many will recognize *Roe v. Wade* as the leading case concerning legal limitations on the availability of abortion.[3] The adjudication of important issues of public policy is not the only business of the American courts, however. In fact, cases involving important issues of public policy statistically are but a small part of the business of the courts. Most civil cases are private disputes of little significance except to the specific plaintiffs and defendants—automobile accident suits; commercial contracts disputes; product safety suits; landlord-and-tenant disputes; divorce and other family legal problems. The American court system also handles millions of criminal cases each year, ranging from prosecutions for murder to parking violations.

An important characteristic of the American legal system is that the same courts and essentially the same procedural rules govern all types of noncriminal litigation. There is a distinct system of procedure in criminal cases, a complex subject that is beyond the scope of this book. Apart from criminal matters, however, the same rules of civil procedure govern great public controversies such as *Brown v. Board of Education* and routine litigation between private parties. Moreover, these controversies generally are adjudicated in the same court systems. There is thus a formal equality—one could say a democratic treatment—of public-issue litigation and ordinary litigation between private parties. Both kinds of litigation are at the same time matters of public interest and of individual justice.

Civil litigation in legally developed political systems has fundamental similarities the world over. Every civil case involves a complaining party who demands a remedy from the courts for an asserted legal wrong. Every case involves a defending party who denies having a legal obligation in the matter, or at least contends that its legal obligation is different or less than the complaining party contends. In any particular case, the facts may be contested, compelling the tribunal to resolve conflicting evidence in making a determination of the facts. In addition, the meaning or application of the law may be contested, in which event the tribunal must resolve conflicting interpretations of the law. Many cases involve disputes of both fact and law. Furthermore, in legal systems based on the Western tradition, the tribunal is in principle indifferent to the social consequences of the outcome of a specific case. The constitutional function of a court is to decide each case according to law and not to rehabilitate the parties or to improve their social consciousness. Concentration on the law and the facts of the specific case reflects the concept that justice should be administered according to law, not according to social necessity. This limitation also means that the courts of civil justice do not remedy all forms of injustice or social wrong. The primary responsibility for remedial social measures lies with other agencies of government, such as the national legislature or executive.

Given these fundamental characteristics of a legal dispute, the procedure for adjudication must meet certain requirements. It must provide an authoritative arbiter to determine the facts and an informed authority to determine the law. According to universally recognized principles of fairness, the arbiter should be neutral as between the parties. So also, the procedure must permit the parties to tender evidence relevant to the factual issues and to suggest sources, such as applicable statutes, that are relevant to the legal issues. The tribunal is obligated to give serious attention to both sides of the dispute, and to all sides if there are more than two parties. The procedure must also have a definite conclusion. Unless there is a principle of finality, the stronger party or the more persistent one can prevail simply by protracting the litigation.

By universally recognized principles of fairness, in most cases there should also be opportunity for appellate review before a higher court. The only exceptions to this principle are in cases involving very small sums of money, where the cost of review would exceed the amount in dispute, and cases involving extraordinary emergency, where some kind of protective relief must be granted to preserve the status quo.

These fundamental similarities among procedural systems can be expressed in simple terminology. A tribunal that has authority to determine a civil controversy is described in American usage as having "jurisdiction of the subject matter" (the word *jurisdiction* derives from Latin roots meaning "the power to say what the law is"). In civil law usage the same concept is called "competence concerning the controversy." A civil case involves issues of fact and issues of law. The plenary hearing where evidence is received is called the "trial" in American usage; in the civil law, it is the "first-instance proceeding." In American usage, a proceeding to review the trial judgement is called an "appeal"; in the civil law a proceeding to review the judgment of a first-instance proceeding is called a "proceeding of the second instance." The principle of finality, in both civil law and American usage, is known as the rule of *res judicata,* meaning "already decided." The concepts of issues of fact and issues of law, trial, appeal, jurisdiction and res judicata are fundamentally similar in the law of all legally developed countries. In this book we focus attention on the distinctive characteristics of American civil procedure. We also contrast American civil procedure with the civil law system of procedure that is employed in Europe, Latin America, and Japan. Contrast, we hope, avoids both idealizing the American system and denigrating it by comparison with an unreal system of perfect justice.

A different version of this book, designed for a European audience, is being published in Italian. The underlying analysis reflects several years of discussion and many written exchanges between us.

GEOFFREY C. HAZARD, JR.
Sterling Professor of Law
Yale University

MICHELE TARUFFO
Professor of Law
University of Pavia

CHAPTER ONE

History

Much of what is now the eastern United States originally was colonized by Great Britain. From the time of the first British settlements in the early seventeenth century, however, colonies were established by other European countries, including the Netherlands (occupying New Amsterdam, which became New York), Sweden (occupying part of what became New Jersey), and France (occupying what became Canada and areas that ranged from what is now western Pennsylvania to New Orleans). From 1660 on, Great Britain aggressively expelled the other European powers, securing what came to be thirteen American colonies as its exclusive domain. These European colonies gradually subjugated, exterminated, or pushed westward the Native Americans (Indians).

In this period, the emerging American legal system became patterned on that of Great Britain. Before 1700, the legal systems of the colonies were relatively primitive, reflecting the condition of early colonial societies, economies, and political structures. Legislation emanated occasionally from governing bodies that resembled town councils more than modern legislatures. The courts and judicial procedure were adaptations of the local tribunals that the settlers had known in English villages. Accordingly, the procedure of the early colonial courts was relatively informal, relying primarily on oral testimony and use of local lay people as arbiters (there were few trained lawyers in the colonies). Historical research indicates, however, that even in the seventeenth century the courts in the colonies occasionally adjudicated complicated controversies concerning such issues as rights in land and the governing powers of churches. In this early period, several characteristics emerged that eventually would become permanent: courts were to be spread throughout the countryside, rather than concentrated in urban centers; courts were to call upon local laymen to determine the facts; and courts were to keep their procedures "simple" and readily intelligible by the ordinary citizen.

In general, the British government was indifferent to the judicial functions performed in the colonies. The legal controversies in the colonial courts usually were of only local and private significance, and hence could be ignored by the central government. However, Great Britain was concerned with legal issues that affected important interests of imperial government, such as the authority of the royal governors of the colonies. To protect these interests, the central government in London, acting through the king's Privy Council, retained authority to review judgments in the colonial courts. Here can be seen in original form a procedure that later came to have constitutional importance. The Privy Council exercised authority to determine whether a proceeding in a colonial court or legislative body conformed to the legal principles recognized in the British imperial regime. This procedure had the following characteristics: review by a judicial body having independent constitutional authority rather than merely an upper-level court of appeal in an integrated judicial system; determination of legal issues of general significance, not evaluation of the specific justice of the judgment in the court below; and resolution of important political issues through judicial proceedings. In embryonic form, the procedure for review of judgments of colonial courts by the English Privy Council resembles the modern American procedure for review of judgments of trial courts by the supreme courts of the various states and by the United States Supreme Court.

The constitutional relationship between the central legal authority and the courts in the colonies was not unique to the British Empire. Those familiar with Spanish history, for example, will recognize the similarity between the Privy Council mechanism of review and the more elaborate system established in Madrid for legal superintendence of Spain's American colonies. The crucial point is that both English and Spanish colonies were components of empires whose central authority, like any other government, was committed to self-preservation. Among the necessary procedures for an imperial government is review of constitutionally important decisions of local courts.

It is paradoxical that this legal aspect of imperialism became a precedent for the authority by which appellate courts in the United States exercise important law-making functions in domestic affairs. The paradox is greater in light of the fact that modern European courts did not exercise any authority over their internal law (as distinct from review of colonial matters) until after World War II, when Europe began to absorb American concepts of constitutional law. The feature of American law that remains most difficult and most important to explain is why a country committed to democratic political and social principles continues to repose important law-making functions in the judicial branch of government.

From about 1700 on, civil litigation in the English colonies came to be more closely patterned on the procedure used in the principal courts of the mother country. This procedure, particularly the common law pleading system, is described later in this chapter. In general, common law procedure was more intricate and required greater technical legal knowledge than earlier colonial legal procedures. Its introduction into the colonies was possible because, as the colonies became more populous and economically more developed, professional judges and lawyers made their appearance: some legally trained officials were sent over by the government in London; other Englishmen with legal training came to seek their fortunes; an increasing number of people born in the colonies went to England for legal training. By 1776, when the War of Independence began, there existed a corps of lawyers familiar with the American versions of common-law procedure.

Although the colonies began cooperating with one another politically as early as 1753 (during the French and Indian War) and established a common voice of protest in the 1770s, their first joint legal act was the Declaration of Independence itself. Until 1776 each colony had sustained a stronger connection with London than with its sister states in matters of government, trade, finance, and law. Each colony developed its own legal institutions around this set of relationships with the mother country. Each colony accordingly had its own court system and judiciary, its own legislation and decisional law, its own legal procedure, and its own legal profession. All of these systems resembled their counterparts in England and hence are appropriately referred to as common law systems. However, the American systems were simplified versions of the originals. For example, although at the time there were separate common law courts in England (notably King's Bench and Common Pleas), in each colony these generally were merged into one tribunal and one procedure.

Each new state remained legally autonomous in the period between the separation from England in 1776 and the adoption of the U.S. Constitution in 1787. Each state regarded itself as a sovereign government within the loose association known as the Confederation. The separate identity of the states that originated in the Revolution continues to have major legal significance, for it is the foundation of the relationship among the fifty states and between each state and the federal government. Even today, the states remain semi-autonomous members of a federation. The federal nature of American government is most apparent in law enforcement, local administration, and judicial institutions. Each state has not only its own governor and legislature but also a separate system of courts and a distinctive procedural law, all stemming from colonial origins.

English Legal Inheritance

The English law of civil procedure, inherited by the new American states in 1776, had accumulated over seven centuries of English constitutional history. Some aspects of English procedure dated back to the Norman invasion of England in 1066; a few, particularly the use of local laymen to determine issues of fact, had even earlier roots. Through this long period, England's legal system had undergone adaptations to meet changing social needs and political conditions. Some changes were accomplished through deliberate legislation, but many were accomplished by the courts through the creation of legal fiction that ascribed new functions to old legal mechanisms.

Taken as a whole, the legal system of eighteenth-century Great Britain could be understood only through practice and memory, not through rational analysis. The English law of procedure had never been subjected to comprehensive revision on the model of the Justinian Code of the sixth-century Roman Empire, or the legal revision that later appeared in Europe in the Napoleonic Codes. The closest approximation of a systematic treatment of English law was Blackstone's *Commentaries on the Common Law,* which was a scholarly treatise, not a legal code. Blackstone did impose a degree of coherence on a largely incoherent body of law, however. Interestingly, his *Commentaries,* first published in 1776, was to have greater influence in the new American states than in Great Britain.

The basic procedural institutions drawn from the English background include:

1. the separation between common law and equity;
2. within the common law, the writ system of procedure;
3. the use of juries for determining issues of fact;
4. the adversary system for presentation of the parties' contentions.

The separation between law and equity, the role of juries, and the adversary system remain salient features of American civil procedure, while the writ system has been superseded by modernized procedure. However, the historic English writ system is the matrix from which the modern American system of procedure has devolved.

The system of civil procedure in effect in the newly independent states of America was therefore, even in 1776, anachronistic and in this sense profoundly conservative. The preservation of an archaic legal system in the new American republics was partly a matter of convenience. In the turmoil of establishing their independence from Great Britain, the states had more pressing political problems than reforming civil procedure. However, preserving the established legal system also had a constitutional motivation. One of the grounds stated in the Declaration of Independence for the separation from England was the colonists' claim that they were entitled to rights of the common law. The common law was perceived to include not only substantive rights but the procedural system in which those rights were embedded. That system was regarded as a fundamental protection of private rights and a source of immunity from government oppression. It would have been a political contradiction for the new states to jettison a legal system that they claimed as a birthright.

The origin and foundation of American civil procedure thus was a system at the same time alien and dearly held. Common law procedure was alien in that it had evolved to deal with problems of civil justice in feudal and postfeudal in England, but then had been implanted in North America, a developing region that had never known feudalism. Common law procedure was dearly held in that its preservation was one of the justifications for overthrowing the English colonial regime. To this day, the right to legal justice according to legal procedure remains a fundamental aspect of the American conception of political justice.

Common Law and the Common Law Courts

At the time of the separation of the colonies from the mother country, the English judicial establishment was an untidy combination of four different central courts and many local courts. The four central courts were King's Bench, Common Pleas, Exchequer, and Chancery. The local courts were innumerable and parochial, including manor courts, village courts, borough courts, and special courts in certain strategic regions within England. The four central courts had the most significance in the ultimate development of American civil procedure, however.

The oldest of the four central courts was King's Bench, which dated back to the twelfth century. King's Bench was the superintending court for enforcing the king's peace and justice. As implied by its name, this court originally was held in the king's presence. Its authority or "jurisdiction" concerned primarily disputes over land, feudal incidents in land, and controversies involving violence and threats of violence. These legal problems—land and violence—were closely related: disputes over land were a principal cause of violence, and use of violence was a means by which local magnates often tried to settle disputes over land.

The king could not always personally attend the proceedings in King's Bench, however. His absence resulted in delay, inconvenience to litigants, and consequent failures of justice. Accordingly, members of the royal legal staff were delegated to hear cases in the king's absence. This arrangement originated as an improvisation but became established as an alternative tribunal, which came to be known as Common Pleas. The Court of Common Pleas had achieved a distinct identity by the thirteenth century.

Over time, the procedures of King's Bench and Common Pleas, though generally similar, became differentiated. At various periods in history, therefore, rights and remedies might be enforceable through one of these courts but not through the other—even though, in a general sense, they were both common law courts.

The third central court, Exchequer, evolved in a somewhat different way. Originally, the exchequer was the king's fiscal office. (Its name derived from the checkerboard tables on which counters, that is, metal disks, were moved about in making financial calculations.) The office resolved disputes between the king and his subjects over amounts due the king for taxes and other exactions. In the feudal system, these exactions often depended on legal relationships between the subject and some third person; accordingly,

the exchequer office came to be involved in resolving disputes between these parties. The authority and procedure of the office became regularized through usage. Upon reaching this stage of development, the fiscal office came to be known as the Court of
Exchequer, having competence over certain kinds of private litigation. The rights enforced in Exchequer overlapped those in the other
common law courts and the procedure differed somewhat.

These three courts—King's Bench, Common Pleas, and Exchequer—were known as common law courts. There is a twofold
significance to the term *common law* as applied to these courts.
The law that they administered was "common" because its authority extended throughout the realm. In this respect they were different from feudal courts and manorial courts, whose judicial authority was based on feudal relationships tied to specific land and
therefore merely local in scope. Thus, *common law* refers to the
king's law as distinct from local law, and hence "the law of the
land."

Common law also signifies that the law administered by these
courts had its origin in decisions of the courts themselves. The law
pronounced by the king's common law courts was distinct from
law pronounced by Parliament through statute, and also distinct
from canon law, which was administered by church courts.

The common law courts' authority to make pronouncements of
law originally derived from a concern to maintain peace within the
realm. Responsibility to maintain peace was expressed in the king's
coronation oath, a responsibility fulfilled through officials whom
the king constituted as judges. In origin, the Court of the King's
Bench was essentially an emergency court, dealing with immediate
violence. The same political concern also underlay the authority of
the courts of Common Pleas and Exchequer.

The jurisprudence of the common law therefore was originally
based upon the wrong of trespass. Trespass by definition is a legal
injury involving "force and violence." More fundamentally, the fact
that the common law courts' competence originally concerned matters of immediate violence provides a legally coherent explanation

why these courts could pronounce law on their own authority. When violence is involved, public necessity requires above all that the status quo be stabilized. The original formulations used in common law procedure were essentially commands that peace be restored, in contemplation that the merits of the controversy could thereafter be examined by more deliberate consideration. By accretions, the common law courts extended their authority not only to address immediate violence but also to adjudicate the underlying legal dispute—for example, right to possession of a specific parcel of real estate—that had given rise to the threat of violence. As royal authority came to dominate that of the lords and squires, the element of violence was reduced to a merely formal aspect of the common law courts' authority. In common law pleading it was still alleged that "force and violence" had been involved, but this was a mere fiction. It was on this basis that the common law courts established their authority to pronounce law as a matter of their own initiative.

By the seventeenth century the inherent authority of the courts in England to declare law was asserted as a basis for restraining royal authority, as well as a basis for giving effect to the king's prerogative. Judicial restraint was imposed on the authority of the king's officials—hence avoiding a direct legal attack on the king himself. These legal concepts evolved along with the resistance in Parliament that culminated in the English Revolution and the English Bill of Rights of 1688. In the eighteenth century these precedents, including the judicially created common law, were invoked by the colonists in asserting their autonomy from king and Parliament.

The authority of common law judges to make law is of course an important element of the American constitutional tradition. In the modern democratic era, that authority is subject to the supervening authority of the legislature, which in turn is subject to the Constitution as interpreted by the judges. However, the authority to reformulate and reshape the law still firmly reposes in American courts.

Common Law Writ Procedure

The basic procedure of the common law courts reflected its origin as a procedure to control violence. A common law suit, called an "action," typically began with a writ. A writ was an order by the king's judicial officials that the defendant take specified steps in response to the wrong described in the writ. Upon taking these steps to restore peace for the time being, the defendant was to answer for his conduct. When the respondent answered, the court could adjudicate both the immediate conduct complained of and the underlying legal dispute from which it had arisen.

Writs in this form were not unique to common law courts or even to England. Similar documents were used in government administration throughout late medieval Europe. The difference in the common law was that there evolved a system of judicial procedure based on the writ. The writ described a wrong consisting of violation of the peace, which in turn was the basis of the court's competence to adjudicate. Since the writ was the foundation of the court's authority to act, the court's competence was directly connected to the nature of the alleged wrong.

Over time, variations of writ were developed called the "forms of action." There was a form of action for recovery of lands claimed by inheritance; another form of action for damages to land resulting from wrongful invasion or use; another for wrongful interference with movable property; another for breach of contract; and so on. The form of action was also the basis for summoning the defendant to respond, for auxiliary remedies such as attachment, and for ultimate enforcement of the judgment. The form of action also determined the defenses that could be interposed by defendant. Thus, common law consisted of various procedures, generally similar but different in detail, corresponding to various substantive legal grievances. Their basic logic nevertheless was the same.

The scope of the writ procedure, originally designed to suppress violence, gradually expanded from the twelfth century to the eighteenth. The definition of acts committed with "force and arms" was extended to include nonviolent conduct having injurious consequences. It was then further extended to include failures to take action. In a leading case in the fourteenth century, the failure of a ferryman to deliver his cargo safely across a river was held to involve "force and arms."[1] The legal wrong involved in the ferryman's case is close to the modern idea of liability for negligence. Although the concept of violence had thus become wholly fictional, it remained the constitutional basis of the common law action.

A similar fiction was the basis of the common law action for breach of contract. The failure to perform on the part of a person who had made a promise was held, by reasoning similar to that in the ferryman's case, to constitute an attenuated form of violence. This basis of legal wrong is close to the modern idea of liability for breach of contract. By these and similar "fictions"—that is, distortions of legal language for the purpose of transforming legal consequences—the common law writ procedure expanded from its basis in preventing violence into a broad jurisprudence of right and remedy.

Under common law procedure, the defendant in principle could deny the complainant's factual allegations or, in the alternative, could dispute that the allegations constituted a legal wrong within the terms of the writ. The first type of defense created an issue of fact; the second created an issue of law. Issues of law were decided by the judges, who in doing so expounded the common law and gradually expanded its scope. In concept, judicial responsibility went no further. That is, the judge's task was not to decide the merits of the case but to decide whether the case stated in the pleadings was valid as a matter of law. If a fact issue was presented, that issue was determined by a jury. Thus, from a very early time common law procedure made a distinction between issues of law and issues of fact that demarcated the functions of the judge and the jury. Aspects of jury trial will be considered throughout this book.

Equity

The fourth central court in England was the Court of Chancery, whose presiding magistrate was the chancellor. The chancellor was the king's general secretary; even today the Lord Chancellor of England exercises administrative duties. From ancient times, certainly as early as the fourteenth century, the chancellor also exercised judicial authority, and in this capacity presided in the Court of Chancery, through which he administered a special remedial justice called equity.

The need for intervention by the chancellor originally arose from limitations on the competence of the common law courts. The common law writs did not cover the full range of legal wrongs, either in concept or in practice. The wrongs over which the common law courts had competence, as we have seen, were defined in terms of an element of violence, actual or nominal. The requirement of violence conceptually excluded wrongs consisting of fraud or breach of faith. In the medieval period, redress for fraud or breach of faith was available in the church courts, but for various reasons this form of redress atrophied. Persons aggrieved by fraud or breach of trust, or who suffered repeated acts of violence, therefore would find that the common law courts provided no remedy, or a remedy that was inadequate on account of delay and technicalities. In desperation they might seek the intervention of the king, invoking his general authority to do justice.

In a case that seemed to call for intervention in the name of justice, the king could order his chief minister, the chancellor, to look into the matter. The chancellor would ask the grievant for a narrative statement of the circumstances. When the allegations appeared meritorious, the chancellor could require the respondent to give his side of the story and, if necessary, could order production of relevant documents and the depositions of witnesses. These measures for producing evidence were carried out by an order known as the *sub poena,* meaning that the witness was "under penalty" of being punished for contempt of court if he did not give his evidence.

A *sub poena duces tecum* is an order to a party or witness to "bring with you" documents or other specified evidentiary material. These terms are still used in American procedure.

On the basis of the evidence so revealed, the chancellor would seek to order a just result in the circumstances—that is, seek to do equity. The procedure in the court of equity was essentially an inquest. In form and substance it was similar to, and to some extent modeled on, the inquests conducted by the church courts. In time, this procedure for extraordinary inquiry by the chancellor became routinized. The grievant's petition was known as a bill in equity, appealing to the discretion of the chancellor and, at the latter's instance, the conscience of the defendant. The bill was both an accusation and a statement of evidence, and its narrative was made on oath. The response was called the answer, also made on oath. Upon having compiled the evidence in this written form, together with evidentiary documents and testimony of witnesses, the chancellor would make an appropriate disposition, called a decree. (The determination of a common law court was called a judgment.) If there was a conflict in testimony, the chancellor could remand the parties to a proceeding in the common law courts, in which the disputed issue could be put to a jury.

The Court of Chancery as a court of equity had three important legal characteristics. First, it did not employ a jury to determine facts. In most instances the court's discovery procedure, by which witnesses and documents were exposed, would yield sufficient evidence to permit a decision. Only in unusual circumstances was it necessary to determine a matter of witness credibility, and in such situations the court could use a jury for the purpose, but only indirectly. Second, the chancellor as judge of the court of equity exercised special discretionary authority to ameliorate the limitations of the common law. This concept, that the judge of a court of equity has unique powers beyond the strict letter of existing law, is another source of independent judicial authority.

Third, the chancellor asserted authority to decide legal controversies according to his conceptions of justice without strict regard to the common law or its procedures. At the beginning of the seventeenth century, during the reign of James I, very broad jurisdictional authority was asserted by Chancellor Ellesmere. However, this claim was contested by the common judges under the leadership of Chief Justice Coke. The Coke-Ellesmere dispute generated intense technical and constitutional argument but eventually lapsed into a détente under which both the common law courts and the court of equity endured. Nevertheless, the argument yielded theories of judicial authority that still echo. Coke's argument was that judges and other ministers of government are bound by the law and only on that basis have authority to pronounce it. Ellesmere's argument, partly reflecting a concept of classical philosophy formulated by Aristotle, was that certain delicate cases require a more equitable form of justice than can be afforded by legal rules. The one argument is that judges uniquely know the law; the other is that judges have unique discretion that transcends the law. The constitutional controversy between common law and equity died out in England but was later revived in the colonies, and from time to time it has reappeared in controversies concerning the right of jury trial in civil cases.

At all events, by the eighteenth century equitable relief from the Court of Chancery could be obtained as a matter of routine in a wide variety of circumstances. These included property transactions tainted by fraud or mistake; breach of trust by fiduciaries, including directors of corporations; instances of threatened wrong not yet committed, such as threats to tear down a building, or to build one on property whose title was in dispute; and refusals to perform contracts calling for sale of specific property, such as land or unique personal property. In theory, the petitioner in equity had to show that his remedy at law was inadequate, thus justifying the intervention of the chancellor. In fact, by the eighteenth century the scope of the common law writs had so expanded that an aggrieved party often could obtain relief for many of these wrongs from the common law courts. Thus, the competence of the common law courts and the court of equity was coextensive to a considerable extent.

By this stage in history, the common law courts and the court of equity had become bureaucratic competitors in the administration of justice. For claims seeking the remedy of damages for overt misconduct, the common law courts had substantially exclusive competence. For claims seeking the remedy of injunction or the uncovering of fraud, the court of equity was a necessary resort. For many other types of wrong, however, the claimant could pursue a writ in the common law courts or a bill in the court of chancery. The claimant's choice often would be determined by the differences in procedure at law and in equity.

These complexities in judicial authority, though functionally archaic in many respects, were the product of practical adaptation to governmental necessity. Through the colonization of North America, these anachronisms, with their complexities, were carried over to the American colonies. By the middle of the eighteenth century, all of the colonies used the complicated common law writ procedure in civil litigation involving claims for damages and in disputes over land ownership. Many of them also had separate courts of equity, in which the procedure by narrative bill was used.

Procedural Differences between Law and Equity

The procedure in equity generally resembled that employed in courts in other parts of Europe at the time and in the courts of most countries today. These features of equity procedure were as follows: The tribunal consisted of a judge without a jury. The court had broad authority to guide the proceedings, including definition of the issues and specification of the evidence. The proceeding began with the grievant's narrative, continued with the defendant's counternarrative, and called forth evidence as directed by the court. The parties' own testimony was competent as evidence; indeed, the aim of the proceeding was often to compel the defendant to make admissions that could reveal wrongdoing. The judge decided legal issues, and usually factual issues as well. The court's final decree would review the evidence, state conclusions of fact, and give reasons for the decision. Were it not for the jury trial guaranty, modern American procedure probably would conform to this model. Indeed, proceedings in administrative agency adjudications—for example, workers' compensation hearings and occupational licensure proceedings—are essentially similar.

Equity procedure in the United States in the nineteenth century acquired another feature, that of appeal, whereby the losing party in the first-instance proceeding could obtain review in a court of second instance. In equity proceedings in England, the first-instance proceeding took place before the chancellor; since the chancellor was the king's chief legal officer, no appeal could be had. Appellate review in equity developed only after first-instance proceedings in equity came to be heard by judges other than the chancellor. This development occurred in the United States by the early nineteenth century and only thereafter in England.

In an appeal from a decree in equity, the whole record of the first-instance trial was open to consideration by the appellate court. In principle and in practice, the appellate court would seek to do justice on the merits and could redetermine the significance of the evidence. An appeal in equity thus was fundamentally similar to second-instance proceedings in other contemporary legal systems.

In most important respects, therefore, the procedure in eighteenth- and early nineteenth-century equity resembled modern litigation in countries other than the United States. The most conspicuous change in equity procedure since the eighteenth century has been in the procedure for receiving the testimony of witnesses. Historically, such testimony in equity was received in the form of written depositions. In the nineteenth century the practice adopted a principle called "orality," so that testimony of witnesses, including the parties, was presented orally. In modern procedure, testimony is received orally except when the witness is unavailable, in which case testimony may be received through written deposition.

Common law procedure in the late eighteenth century was in many respects quite different from that in equity. The writ system of pleading required stylized allegations in the antique formulae of the writs rather than a narrative of the facts. Testimony fully revealing the facts was not forthcoming until trial. Trial of fact issues took place before a jury; a jury would be convened only when an issue of fact was produced at the pleading stage, which was conducted at the court in London. In many types of action, the jury trial was held in the county where the disputed transaction had arisen. The writ system correspondingly maintained a sharp distinction between issues of law, which were for the court, and issues of fact, which were decided by the jury. There was no procedure by which parties could obtain documents or other evidence from an opposing party. Hence, there was no disclosure of evidence until the jury was seated, whereupon each party had to rely on proof it could marshal for itself. Moreover, the litigants and others having a direct interest in the controversy were incompetent to testify; testimonial evidence was available only from nonparty witnesses.

The common law's distinction between law and fact approximately corresponds to the boundary in modern procedure between the functions of the judge and of the jury. The judge and the jury each speak with the voice of "justice" but represent different modes of justice. The judge is the voice of positive or "official" law, historically emanating from the authority of the king. This authority is expressed in the general legal rules of the judge's charge to the jury. In contrast, the jury is the voice of "the country," meaning the general citizenry as represented in the jury. Theirs is the authority of the community at large, translating the law's generalizations into a determination about the specific circumstances of the case.

The distinction between issues of fact and issues of law was also maintained insofar as appellate review was afforded. Indeed, until the nineteenth century there was no appeal procedure in common law. The absence of appeal was a logical corollary of common law procedural theory. In the concept of the common law, the legal issues were addressed at the pleading stage and resolved by argument held before all the judges of the court. If resolution of the legal issue determined the case, no trial of fact issues was necessary.

By the same token, going to trial on the facts signified that the legal issues had already been resolved. All that remained for decision was the jury's verdict as to the facts, rendered under instruction by the judge concerning the legal standard the jury was to apply. Any defect in the verdict therefore would necessarily be the result of error in the way in which the trial was conducted, or misbehavior of some kind on the part of the jury in arriving at its verdict. In concept, therefore, subsequent consideration of a case decided by jury verdict was an inquest about the jury trial itself, not a reconsideration of the merits of the case.

Hence, in common law procedure a second-instance proceeding was not a retrial of the parties' dispute but a trial of the first-instance trial. Important vestiges of this concept remain embedded in modern American civil procedure. An appeal in American procedure primarily inquires whether the first-instance proceeding was conducted according to correct legal principles and was uncontaminated by irregularity, not whether the first-instance judgment was the right outcome. This distinction corresponds to that between issues of law, which are within the competence of the appellate court to determine authoritatively, and issues of fact. As to the issues of fact, the determination of the first-instance court ordinarily is conclusive if the proceedings were correctly conducted.

Of course, in practice the distinction between law and fact cannot be clearly maintained. The attempt to do so has produced endless obscurities and casuistries in procedural reasoning. Nevertheless, the concept remains that there is a fundamental distinction between law and fact, marking the division of function between judge and jury and also between appellate and trial court.

In addition to differences in procedure between common law and equity, there were some differences in the substantive legal principles applied in the two systems. For example, the common law refused to provide redress for certain kinds of misrepresentation in contract negotiation, particularly affirmations that were erroneous but not knowingly fraudulent. The court of equity would rescind contracts that had resulted from such misrepresentations. A further example is that equity recognized the right of stockholders in a business corporation to bring suit against the directors in cases of gross mismanagement, while none of the common law writs covered this kind of wrong. There were many such differences. Taken together, they resulted in a body of legal principles in equity that was distinct from those in common law. Hence, litigation in equity not only was conducted by procedure different from common law but also could be determined by different legal rules.

This very complicated system was transplanted largely intact into many of the colonies, which thereafter became the new states. The states of Delaware and New Jersey perpetuated separate courts of common law and of equity, each having its own judges and its own procedure based on the English models. The state of New York established a different structure, in which there was a single first-instance court of comprehensive competence that employed two different procedures, depending on whether the case was in law or in equity. Some states had a single court and a single procedure based on the common law, but applied equitable principles in cases such as those involving fraud or mistake. Moreover, American common law procedure, while simplified from that used in the mother country, nevertheless perpetuated many technical anachronisms.

The Adversary System

A basic feature of modern American procedure is the adversary system, in which initiative and responsibility for presentation of the case rests primarily with advocates on behalf of the parties. It is the function of the advocate for the plaintiff to analyze the facts and legal basis of the grievance which will be sued on; to select the appropriate legal concept for presenting the case—in the common law system, determining which writ should be used; to gather before trial the evidence to be presented in support of the case; at trial, to present the evidence by questioning the appropriate witnesses and offering relevant documents; and, at the conclusion of trial, to argue to the trier of fact (judge or jury) that the evidence should lead to a finding for the plaintiff. The advocate for the defendant has corresponding responsibilities. The defense must anticipate the legal contentions and the evidence to be offered by the plaintiff, and present countering evidence at trial. At trial, counsel for each side is permitted to cross-examine witnesses presented by the opposing party.

The adversary system should be contrasted with the judge-centered procedure used in most modern legal systems, including those of continental Europe and Japan. These are based on the civil law, hence called the civil law system. The civil law system had its historic origin in the Justinian Code formulated by the Roman emperor in the sixth century and carried forward through the canon law of the Roman Catholic church and a scholastic legal tradition in the medieval and Renaissance periods. This body of substantive and procedural law was reformulated following the French Revolution into the Civil Code, also called the Napoleonic Code, and rapidly promulgated throughout Western Europe and Latin America. The Civil Code was designed to clarify and rationalize the legal system, synthesizing all legal principles into a concise code that could be universally understood.

The constitutional theory of the Civil Code reflects the political aspirations of the Enlightenment and the French Revolution. These aspirations included the ideas that legal rules should be exclusively expressed in the statutory pronouncements of the legislature, as the voice of the people. The task of the courts is to ascertain the rules and apply them to specific cases; the task of the judge is to guide the reception of evidence revealing the matter in dispute; and the task of the advocates is to assist the judge in this ministerial task.

The theory of the civil law system precludes judicial law making, even in the guise of "interpretation," and it presumes that the truth in court is objectively determinable and not merely a pragmatic choice between conflicting versions. The judge is supposed to know the law and therefore to know what evidence is relevant and how to orchestrate the production and evaluation of evidence. Hence, in theory and to a large extent in practice, procedural initiative in the civil law system lies with the judge, whereas procedural initiative in the common law system lies with the advocates. Hence the term *adversary system*.

The use of the adversary system in jury trials was a relatively late development in England. In the early development of the common law writ system, the parties usually had advocates at the pleading stage of an action. However, the function of the jury originally was that of a collective witness. The jurors were selected from the place where the dispute arose and would have knowledge of the facts, either direct information or that acquired by common account. They drew on their collective knowledge to give a verdict. In such a procedure, there would be little use for advocates to present the evidence.

Over time, however, the jury's function shifted from that of evidence-givers to that of neutral assessors of evidence provided by others. This transformation appears not to have been complete until the late seventeenth or eighteenth century. Apparently it was in this same period that trial advocates came to be generally employed in jury trials. The inference is that by then a jury was expected to determine the case on the basis of evidence presented to it; that gathering the evidence was not a responsibility of the judges, who were concerned only with pleadings and with the verdict; that parties gathered and presented evidence for themselves, but discovered the usefulness of expert assistance; and that lawyers could provide the necessary expert assistance. The historical evidence of this development, however, is fragmentary.

In any event, the jury system was established at the birth of the United States and the adversary system was established with it. The adversary system was also employed in equity, where its use does not appear to have been so necessary.

The judge in the adversary system has a relatively passive role, but nevertheless performs important functions. These include: supervising the seating of a jury from among the citizens summoned for jury duty; at the beginning of trial, describing to the jury the general nature of the case and their responsibilities in deciding issues of fact; acting as umpire in the course of the trial, to restrain the advocates from pursuing irrelevancies or becoming overzealous; after all the evidence has been received, giving instructions to the jury about the legal principles to be applied in reaching a verdict; and, after the trial is over, considering whether there were mishaps at trial so prejudicial that a retrial should be held.

In practice, many judges perform a much more active role, including general direction of discovery, active questioning during trial, and giving of interim explanations to the jury. The roles of advocate and judge in the development and presentation of a case are more fully explored in chapters 5, 6, and 7.

Code Pleading

The separate procedural systems in common law and equity continued in existence in the United States for many years following establishment of the Constitution of 1787. The dual system was also adopted for the federal courts created under the Constitution and was maintained in a few states until the latter half of the twentieth century. However, at the beginning of the nineteenth century a reform movement developed to simplify the procedural system. The fruits of this movement came to be known as code pleading.

The impetus to reform the dual system of law and equity was both conceptual and practical. Conceptually, code-pleading reform rested on the premise that law should be understandable as a matter of common intelligence, rather than being an occult historical science. If made intelligible to reason, law would be accessible to the mind of every citizen. This democratic principle, also expressed in the European civil codes, applied to procedural law as well. Hence, the law of procedure should be made clear, simple, and logical. The code-pleading reform of procedure was thus a child of the Enlightenment and Utilitarian philosophy, so congenial to the American mind. The philosophy of the Enlightenment invited the formulation of procedure on the basis of rational analysis of the human condition, rather than upon historical tradition. Utilitarian philosophy seemed to provide a guiding principle—the greatest good for everyone, considered as equals before the law—in terms of which rational analysis could proceed.

The practical impetus for the reform of American civil procedure arose from the many dysfunctional aspects of the inherited system. No purpose was served by maintaining two systems of procedure, a duality which was an accident of English history. No purpose was served by maintaining the various kinds of common law writs, a complexity which was also an accident of English history. No purpose was served by maintaining the technical formulations and legal fictions in which procedural rules had come to be expressed, both in common law and in equity. It was believed, to a large degree correctly, that these anachronisms resulted in failures of justice. It was also believed that they entrenched lawyers in control of the courts, for only lawyers could understand the system's intricacies. Thus, the movement to code pleading was a political as well as a legal reform.

Perhaps the more interesting question about the code-pleading reform is why it took so long in coming. The reform was not generally adopted in the state legal systems until after 1850, and was fully adopted in the federal courts only in 1938. The American democratic ideal requires that law, including legal procedure, should be readily intelligible to the ordinary citizen. The New World was envisioned as fashioned by the human mind, freed from the bondage of history. Such a political philosophy would put radical reform of judicial procedure high on the political agenda after the Revolution.

However, as we have seen, the common law, despite its technical intricacy, was understood to be a constitutional protection. The very principle of constitutionalism entails the conservative premise that legal rules once adopted should not be superseded except for good reason and upon general assent, even if they result in temporary inconvenience and injustice. American independence had been achieved in the name of such a constitutional theory. Hence,

American political tradition combined a legally conservative component that argued against radical change in the received legal system, including the system of procedure.

Nevertheless, the reform of civil procedure emerged in the wake of the transition to Jacksonian democracy in the early nineteenth century. The term *code* refers to the fact that the reform was accomplished by comprehensive statutory change, not by gradual modification through judicial decision. The term *pleading* refers to the fact that the new rules centered on the statement of claims, which were to be set forth in documents referred to as pleadings. The code-pleading system was devised in New York and was widely known as the Field Code after its principal draftsman, David Dudley Field, a New York lawyer. After its adoption in New York in 1848, the code-pleading system was soon adopted in California and most of the midwestern and western states, where the conservative legal tradition was less deeply rooted. Most of the New England states and those along the Atlantic coast continued to adhere to the old system until the twentieth century.

The principal features of the code-pleading system were as follows: First, the distinction between law and equity was abolished, except for preservation of jury trial. Hence, a single system of civil procedure replaced the common law writs and the equity bill. Second, statements of claim and motions were required to be in simple and direct language, abandoning the anachronistic formulations of the old systems. Third, in principle all claims arising from the transaction in dispute between two parties could be presented in one case. It was no longer necessary to use one action to obtain the common law remedy of damages and a separate action to obtain equitable remedies such as injunction. Fourth, the codes soon abolished the common law rule that parties were incompetent as witnesses. Henceforth, parties could testify on the same basis as independent witnesses. Finally, in a limited way the equitable procedure for discovery was made available in actions for damages. As noted earlier, at common law there was no discovery of an opposing party's evidence until trial.

Taken as a whole, the code-pleading reform was a brilliant success. Not only was it widely adopted by the states for their courts, but also, through a sequence to be described in the following section, it governed many types of cases in the federal courts. Moreover, the objectives of the reform were largely if not completely accomplished. Pleading of claims was much simpler. With further reforms in the twentieth century it was possible to bring into one proceeding all interested parties involved in a complicated legal controversy. Discovery, although limited, enabled litigants to obtain vital documents from an opposing party. In accordance with the common law tradition, jury trial was preserved in cases involving claims for damages and those concerning land titles.

The system was not completely simple, however. Habits of technicality among judges and lawyers persisted, particularly in administering the rules governing pleading and the joining of parties. The new rules inevitably acquired their own technicalities as well. A lawsuit is a power struggle by the parties as well as a search for justice by the court. In the legal power struggle, advocates for the parties have both the incentive and the duty to gain advantage through procedural maneuver, and the incentive is especially strong in a case whose merits are weak. In resolving this partisan struggle, reference must be made to rules of procedure, which, like all legal rules, are technical at the margins of their meaning. Many specific procedural disputes cannot be resolved by a general principle of "procedural fairness." On the contrary, the pressure of the legal power struggle forces the judges in any procedural system to make decisions that often involve "legalistic" distinctions.

For example, the code-pleading rule required the plaintiff's complaint to be "plain and direct." But how much specific detail in the plaintiff's narrative does this standard require? Resolving that issue generated complicated technical distinctions between "facts" and "conclusions." The code-pleading rule required that all claims should relate to the "same subject matter." But what events constitute a subject matter and how close a relationship is required with other events so that the latter can be considered the "same"?

Resolving that issue generated complicated distinctions as well. The evolving jurisprudence of code pleading generated many other such distinctions.

Over time, many of these distinctions became as complicated as those in the common law writ system. There were other problems that the code-pleading system failed to resolve satisfactorily. For example, distinctions remained, even under the codes, between "actions at law" and "suits in equity," apart from the problem of jury trial. Discovery was limited to information "necessary" to the case, but a party seeking discovery often could not tell whether the information was necessary without first seeing it. There remained impediments to joining all parties involved in a complicated legal controversy. These and other difficulties remained embedded in the code-pleading system through 1938.

The Federal Rules of Civil Procedure

The U.S. Constitution, adopted in 1787, authorized establishment of a system of federal courts independent of the courts of the states. The principal objectives in establishing an independent system of federal courts were twofold. First, federal courts could be expected to be more sympathetic in enforcing the federal government's interests than the state courts had been. Second, federal courts could be more disinterested in litigation between citizens of different states than the state courts had been. Accordingly, the new federal first-instance courts were endowed with competence in cases involving the government and in those in which the parties were citizens of different states.

It was generally understood that the federal courts could have their own distinct system of civil procedure. However, there were important practical obstacles to devising such a system. A major difficulty arose from the federal nature of the new government. As described earlier, each state had its own procedural system, although the systems bore a family resemblance to each other. It was therefore convenient to provide that the federal trial courts in each state should use the common law procedural system of that state. Such was the provision of a statute adopted during the first sitting of the Congress of the United States in 1789, known as the Conformity Act.

However, conforming the procedure in federal trial courts to that of local state procedure was impracticable in proceedings in equity. As noted above, some of the states did not have separate equity procedure. Yet the federal trial courts, called the district and circuit courts, had competence equivalent to the English courts of equity. What procedure should be used in such cases? The solution adopted in the 1789 legislation was that, in equity proceedings, the federal courts should follow the procedure traditionally employed in equity courts. Hence, in the original federal procedural system the distinction was maintained between law and equity, although both were administered in the same courts. The "law side" of the court used the common law procedure of the state in which the federal court was located; the "equity side" used the bill-and-deposition procedure of the English Court of Chancery.

This mixed system prevailed in the federal courts until 1938. It caused much difficulty, chiefly because it required that federal civil litigation vary in its procedural aspects from one state to another. Moreover, in many states the common-law procedure—which the federal courts were required to employ on the "law side"—was very antiquated. Federal courts of the twentieth century found themselves applying legal technicalities that emanated from the eighteenth century and earlier.

In response to these difficulties—after many years of debate— Congress adopted the Enabling Act of 1934, which authorized promulgation of a single civil procedural system for the federal courts. The responsibility for formulating the new rules was conferred on the U.S. Supreme Court, with a proviso that the rules be submitted to Congress for approval. The Supreme Court delegated the drafting task to a committee composed of experienced legal scholars, judges, and lawyers from various parts of the country, employing Dean Charles Clark of Yale Law School as draftsman.

The committee's draft, after discussion and revision, was submitted and adopted in 1938.

This procedural system is the Federal Rules of Civil Procedure, still in effect today with several subsequent amendments. Since 1938, most states on their own initiative have revised their procedural codes on the model of the Federal Rules. Hence, from 1789 to 1938, federal procedure principally conformed to state procedure, but since 1938 state procedure has come principally to conform to federal procedure. When reference is made today to American civil procedure, whether in comparative law or in law school instruction, it is the Federal Rules that usually are in contemplation.

Generally speaking, the reforms made in the Federal Rules consisted of further adoption of the principles of equity procedure. Primary among these was greater liberalization of discovery. The discovery provisions of the Federal Rules enable an inquiring party to ask questions through pretrial deposition, and to demand production of documents before trial, concerning any matter "relevant to the subject of the action." Furthermore, the discovery rules permit obtaining such material whether or not it consists of admissible evidence. Thus, for example, hearsay statements can be obtained. Another change effected in the Federal Rules was the relaxation of the pleading rules. The Federal Rules concerning pleading permit a party to proceed with an action, including discovery, upon a very general statement of a grievance. The Federal Rules also liberalized the rules of joining parties, including the procedure for class actions. The Federal Rules of Civil Procedure are discussed more fully in subsequent chapters.

CHAPTER TWO

The Legal System and the
Structure of Government

The law of civil procedure governs the adjudication of legal disputes between private parties—for example, litigation over contracts, property, and civil wrongs. The bulk of civil litigation involves controversies of this kind. In the American legal system, except for criminal matters, the law of civil procedure also governs the adjudication of public law controversies. These include litigation over the constitutionality of legislation, the legality of conduct by government officials, and the scope of authority conferred on administrative and regulatory agencies—that is, legal aspects of the exercise of public authority, hence "public law."

The central role of ordinary courts in resolving public law issues is unique to the United States. In most other modern political systems, issues of public law are usually resolved in special courts having jurisdiction of administrative or constitutional questions and using special procedure for determining such questions. In the United States these questions are resolved in the same courts that have jurisdiction over ordinary litigation between private parties, and according to the same procedure used in ordinary litigation. A controversy over public law typically originates in a dispute between a private party and a governmental agency, and usually will first be considered within the agency itself. However, the controversy can then be carried into the courts by appeal from the agency or by a suit against the agency officials. Thus, legal questions such as those concerning racial discrimination by government agencies, abortion carried out in public hospitals or with public funding, and police handling of arrests can all be presented in the form of an ordinary civil lawsuit. Civil procedure thereby is the medium for presenting legal claims of social, political, and economic justice, and the courts are the immediate arbiter of the issues, sometimes their ultimate arbiter.

Comprehending the function of American civil justice therefore requires attention to the relationship between the American legal system and the American structure of government. That structure is organized upon two basic principles: separation of powers and federalism. Both of these principles are constitutional, being established in the Constitution of the United States and corresponding constitutions of each of the states.

Separation of Powers

The American national government is based on the separation of powers: the legislative power, exercised by Congress; the executive power, exercised by the President; and judicial power, exercised by the Supreme Court and the lower federal courts. The states have similar internal structures of government: a bicameral legislature (except in Nebraska) composed of bodies usually designated as the Assembly and Senate; an executive called the governor; and a state court system headed by a state supreme court. (In New York the highest court is called the Court of Appeals.)

The legislature at both the federal and state levels has exclusive authority as against the other branches of government to enact statutes, including tax legislation, regulatory measures, and criminal prohibitions. The executive has authority to propose legislation and a power to veto legislation that can be overridden only by an exceptional majority in the legislature. The executive also has general supervision of much of the daily business of government, including fiscal and personnel administration. State government also creates and regulates local government organization, including cities, counties, and special-purpose bodies such as school districts.

Each level of government has a large number of administrative and regulatory agencies. These have been created to govern specific subject matter such as health, education, and tax assessment and collection. The states have all kinds of local government bodies, such as public hospital corporations, irrigation districts, and fire protection districts. Both the states and the federal government have local branch offices of their respective administrative agencies: for example, driver's license bureaus of state government and the Labor Department of the federal government.

The federal court system and the court systems of the states are described more fully below.

All these governmental branches and agencies, including the legislature and the courts themselves, are constituted by legal rules. Some of these rules are prescribed in constitutional provisions: for example, Article I of the U.S. Constitution, which establishes Congress; Article II, which establishes the Presidency; and the reference in Article III to the U.S. Supreme Court. There are counterpart provisions in state constitutions. These provisions are augmented and implemented by statutory provisions. For example, many functions of Congress are governed by statute; most powers exercised by the President are conferred by statute; the whole lower federal court system is established by statute; all the administrative agencies at the federal level and most at the state level are created and given their powers in statutes enacted by the legislature. The administrative agencies at federal and state level have authority, subordinate to the legislation by which the agencies have been established, to adopt regulations in their domain. Administrative regulations augment the statutes and generally have the same force as statutory law.

Statutes enacted by the legislature and regulations adopted by administrative agencies create legal powers and responsibilities of government officials. They also may create rights and duties for private citizens and private organizations, rights and duties which govern relations both with the government and with one another. For example, a speed limit creates a legal duty that may be enforced by the police resulting in a criminal penalty; the same speed limit may be the basis of a claim of negligent driving in a suit for damages by an injured victim against the delinquent motorist. For further example, statutes impose requirements for public filing of relevant information in various kinds of financial transactions and also impose civil liability on a seller who fails to provide truthful information to the buyers in such transactions.

The rules creating branches and agencies of government are called organic or constitutive rules. The rules creating powers, responsibilities, duties, and liabilities can be called regulatory rules. Both kinds of rules may call for interpretation and application. Under the principle of separation of powers, it has become established that the courts have the final authority to determine the meaning and application of constitutional and statutory provisions that are drawn into legal controversy. Thus, government agencies and officials have only such authority as is conferred by law, and the courts have authority to determine what the law has conferred.

Two corollaries of this principle are also established. First, no branch of government legally may act beyond the scope of powers conferred on it by the constitution—the U.S. Constitution as regards the branches of the federal government, and the state constitution as regards branches of that state's government. An action going beyond these constitutional limits is deemed *ultra vires,* "beyond power," and hence legally invalid. Second, an official who acts ultra vires—in excess of constitutional limitations or of authority conferred by law—is generally subject to direct legal attack in the form of a suit for an injunction to prevent the official from acting, or for damages if a private person is injured as a result of such action. Thus it is that a government official who acts beyond the powers of office, as finally determined by the courts, can be held directly accountable in the courts. In some contexts the law of criminal procedure will be involved. For example, it can be a defense to criminal prosecution that law enforcement officials exceeded their authority in maintaining the prosecution.

The principal procedure for determining legal accountability is that used in the ordinary courts. Thus, the law of civil procedure governs not only litigation between private parties over such matters as contract, property, and negligence, but also litigation involving the interpretation of statutes and regulations and the validity of governmental action taken under color of statutes and regulations. The logic is as follows: (1) the principle of separation of powers requires that the legislature not act beyond its constitutional authority, and that executive officials not act beyond the powers conferred on them by statute or constitutional provision; (2) the principle of separation of powers also establishes the courts as the final legal arbiter of that principle; (3) an official who acts beyond his or her legal authority acts unlawfully and is subject to legal liability accordingly; (4) legal liability is imposed through injunction, and sometimes damages actions, obtainable by ordinary lawsuit; (5) ordinary lawsuits are within the jurisdiction of the ordinary courts and are governed by the law of civil procedure; and (6) the law of civil procedure regulates how the constitutional principle of separation of powers is given legal effect at the point of the law's immediate administration.

To Americans the outcome of this logic, if not the logic itself, is familiar: Everyone knows a policemen can be sued for beating up someone unjustifiably, and that a zoning board can be sued if it refuses to apply the building regulations properly. However, the whole framework of premises supporting this common knowledge is quite different from that in most other modern nations, although in several (notably Israel) there is a somewhat similar relationship between civil litigation and the exercise of governmental authority. Most modern nations have a parliamentary structure in which legislative and executive authority are fused and provide general policy guidance to the permanent administrative apparatus of government. Conduct of government officials that is ultra vires or unlawful is treated as an aspect of administration rather than as a matter for adjudication in the ordinary civil courts. As an aspect of administration, such conduct is subject to adjudication in special courts of administrative justice, using special procedures and providing special remedies of correction and restitution. In the parliamentary system the improper action of an official does not diminish the official's legal status as such, nor does it result in a private legal wrong. In the United States, constitutional theory gives a central place to the courts and to litigation in the ordinary functions of government.

Federalism

The United States has a federal structure of government, consisting of the national government and fifty states. The states are subordinate to the national government but have broad governmental authority in their own spheres. The terms of this subordination and the scope of state governmental authority are defined by legal rules, constitutional and statutory. These rules are often the basis of legal contentions presented in civil litigation and adjudicated by the courts.

As we have seen in chapter 1, the states existed as colonies prior to the American Revolution and as substantially independent sovereignties between the Revolution and the adoption of the Constitution in 1787. The Constitution created the federal government and defined its powers, leaving to the states the residual authority not delegated to the federal government. The states continue to have general powers of governance, including such matters as public education, corporation and commercial law, contract and property law, and the basic legal obligations of citizens to one another. The states also retain authority over family law and the transmission of property at death, including administration of decedents' estates.

However, the powers of the federal government are substantial and have expanded over the course of the nation's history. Today they include conducting foreign relations and national defense; regulating foreign and interstate commerce; establishing the monetary system and regulating banking; maintaining the postal service; supervising interstate transportation and the telecommunications system; raising money by taxation, such as the income tax; and spending money for public welfare, including health care, education, development of science, and subsidization of industries such as agriculture.

The original conception of the federal government's authority was much more modest. In the early years of the United States, the national government was primarily concerned with foreign relations, development of the territory west of the Appalachian mountains, and compromising the question of slavery. Over the last two centuries the federal sphere has grown by accretion, largely as a result of economic development and political evolution, but also through legal change. The legal changes include constitutional amendment; expansive judicial interpretation of constitutional language, particularly the power to regulate "commerce among the several states"; and congressional implementation of expanded constitutional authority by statutory enactments and administrative regulation. Most aspects of business and financial transactions and many aspects of the functions of state and local government are now intensively regulated by federal law.

Within its sphere of authority, the federal government is legally superior to the states. This relationship is expressed in the Supremacy Clause of the Constitution, according to which federal law is the "supreme Law of the Land."[1] The Supremacy Clause specifically obligates all judges, including those of the state courts, to give effect to the superior position of federal law. Hence, not only federal judges but state judges as well are required to apply federal law where state law has been superseded. For example, the requirements of a federal statute regulating pension funds, the environment, and securities transactions must be given effect in place of preexisting state legal rules on the same subject. These federal requirements often impose obligations on private persons that can be enforced through civil lawsuits. In such litigation, whether in federal or state court, federal law is applied.

The Constitution imposes other limitations on state autonomy. State courts are required to assume jurisdiction of claims based on federal law and to give effect to legal defenses established by federal law, even where the federal law is inconsistent with state public policy. The Contract Clause in the original Constitution makes invalid any state law that would "impair" the obligation of contracts. More significant is the Fourteenth Amendment, adopted after the Civil War, which broadly prohibits the states from depriving any person of due process of law or equal protection of law. The Due Process Clause has been held to require, for example, that in state court proceedings the parties as a general rule must be given written notice in advance of hearing and the opportunity to present evidence and legal argument at a trial.[2] The Equal Protection Clause requires, for example, that state law not make invidious differentiations among citizens on the basis of such characteristics as race, gender, or economic position.[3]

The Constitution also imposes legal obligations on the states in their relationships with each other. The Privileges and Immunities Clause requires the courts of a state to accord to citizens of other states the same procedural rights as its own citizens enjoy, such as the right to retain legal counsel and the right to jury trial. The Full Faith and Credit Clause requires the courts of a state to recognize and give effect to judgments entered in the courts of a sister state. Principles of constitutional law also limit the extent to which the courts of a state may require nonresidents to respond to litigation based on transactions that arose outside the state. Thus, a resident of New York cannot be summoned into a California court to litigate a controversy having no connection to California.[4]

The intricate ways in which federal law pervades ordinary legal relationships can be suggested through an illustration. Suppose a citizen of New York purchased goods from a Texas seller and that a dispute then arose concerning obligations in the transaction. The New York citizen would have a federally guaranteed right to sue in the Texas state courts; the Texas seller would have a corresponding right of access to the New York courts. If the Texas seller brought suit in the Texas court, the obligation of the New York defendant to respond would be determined primarily by federal constitutional law. Each court would also be required under federal principles to take due account of the other state's law if there was doubt as to which state's law governed the transaction. If the transaction itself involved an aspect that was governed by federal law, the courts of both states would be obliged to apply the federal law. If the suit went to judgment in either state, as a matter of federal law it must be enforced in the other state.

The federal system therefore involves not only the political relationship between the federal government and the states but a complex web of legal rules. These rules govern both the vertical relationships between the federal government and the states and various horizontal relationships between the states. Taken together this body of law is a complex, esoteric jurisprudence; any part of it can become involved in almost any civil case.

Sources of Law

At both the federal level and state levels, the courts derive their decisions from three basic sources: constitutional law, legislation, and common law. Among these, constitutional law is supreme, legislation is the next most authoritative, and common law is authoritative only in the absence of constitutional or legislative provisions.

The U.S. Constitution is authoritative in all legal matters to which it pertains. As we have seen, it not only establishes the three branches of government at the federal level but also has many provisions limiting the powers of the states and guaranteeing the rights of individuals. Notable among individual rights guaranteed by the Constitution are those clustered around the rubric of due process. The Fifth Amendment, a part of the Bill of Rights adopted in 1791, provides that no person "be deprived of life, liberty or property without due process of law." This guaranty applies against the federal government. A parallel provision in the Fourteenth Amendment, adopted in 1868, imposes a similar limitation against activities of state and local governments. The Fourteenth Amendment's requirement of equal protection expressly governs the states and the same principle has been held by implication to apply to the federal government. The requirement of equal protection, for example, has been held to prohibit litigants in civil cases from discriminating against racial minorities in the selection of juries.

Two other important provisions of the Constitution having direct significance in civil litigation were noted in the preceding section. One is the Full Faith and Credit Clause, which requires that full recognition be given by each state to the laws and judgments of other states.[5] Hence, the rights established by a judgment in a civil action in one state generally must be given effect in other states without reexamination of the merits of the controversy. Historically, this provision has strongly influenced the legal unification of the country, mitigating the fact that the states have separate legal systems. The second provision is the Supremacy Clause, which provides that the U.S. Constitution and federal laws and treaties have superior authority to state law, and requires state judges to abide by the Constitution. Particularly in the early years after the founding of the federal government, this provision had important influence in establishing the legal authority of the federal government in ordinary legal matters. The principle of the Supremacy Clause— that federal law has superior authority in matters that it addresses— remains a cornerstone of the American legal system, including its system of civil procedure.

Another significant provision of the Constitution is the guaranty of a jury trial in civil cases. This provision does not apply to the states, but most state constitutions have similar guaranties. The right of jury trial and its significance are considered in chapter 7.

State constitutions contain provisions defining the structure of their respective court systems, so that the judiciary in most states has a constitutional foundation independent of the legislature. State constitutions also contain guaranties of individual rights that in many respects are more protective than the counterpart provisions of the U.S. Constitution. Thus, many state constitutions have their own due process and equal protection clauses, which in many instances confer fuller rights on individuals than the Fourteenth Amendment. Moreover, many state constitutions provide that the courts "shall always be open." Provisions such as this have been interpreted to require that civil cases be open to the public and to the news media.

The second legal source of American law is legislation. Subject to the limitations of the U.S. Constitution and of the constitutions of the individual states, the legislature has supreme legal authority. A statute governing a subject that was previously determined by common law therefore supersedes the common law. For example, commercial law in the United States originally was common law but now is embodied in the Uniform Commercial Code, a comprehensive statute adopted by many states that governs transactions involving the sale of goods. Related to legislation are administrative regulations. These are supplemental rules adopted by government agencies pursuant to legislative authorization. Government supervision of such activities as banking, the securities markets, and workplace safety is carried out largely by administrative regulation.

The third source of law is common law, often called decisional law. This consists of the accumulated body of pronouncements of the law by the courts in the course of deciding cases. As we have seen in chapter 1, the common law was derived from England, where its legal basis was the authority of the king's judges to decide legal disputes in which the king's interest or responsibility was involved. These decisions were considered authoritative for the future and therefore in subsequent cases were treated as definitive legal interpretations. Decision in one case was precedent for later cases, and later cases could reiterate, modify, or extend earlier pronouncements. Over time, this cyclical process established the system of precedent. The common law thus became a self-regenerating body of decisional law, pronounced on the authority of the judiciary.

Prior to the English settlement of America in the seventeenth century, these decisions aggregated into a broadly comprehensive *corpus juris*. The body of law included rules concerning property, civil wrongs, contract obligations, and other subjects. In the colonization of America, these legal principles were a part of the settlers' cultural heritage, for the colonists brought the common law with them and applied it as "their law." In providing for court systems, the state constitutions directed the judges to apply the common law except to the extent that it was inconsistent with the state constitutions or legislation, or with the special conditions of the American situation. These clauses were known as reception provisions because they "received" the common law into the new states.

The reception provisions adopted not only the content of the common law but the common law decisional process itself. By implication they authorized the courts of the states to continue the process of regenerating the common law. An additional element of judicial activism stemmed from the fact that many details of the common law had to be modified to function satisfactorily in the American environment. A famous example was the rule governing liability for crop damage caused by straying cattle. The English common law rule was that the owner of cattle had to "fence in" the herd to prevent injury to neighbors. This rule seemed inappropriate in many of the Western states, where the range was wide and the crop lands relatively few. Hence, some American courts held that the crop owner had to "fence out" other people's cattle or bear the damage. Even more boldly, in the early nineteenth century the American courts felt empowered to pronounce legal concepts which they considered gave better expression to democratic principles than did the rules inherited from England. By way of justification, these forms of judicial lawmaking were considered not to contradict general popular sentiment, but to give it voice. Thus, the anciently founded premise that common law judges may expound the law was given legitimacy on a different basis.

The common law is a body of legal rules that can be synthesized into textual forms similar to statutes and to the civil codes of European countries. Treatises on legal subjects perform this synthesis, taking the judicial decisions as authoritative sources. In this form the rules of the common law textually are similar to those of legal systems based on statute, such as the European civil law system. In constitutional concept, however, the common law is an accumulation of decisions that judges interpret and adapt as conditions change, subject to the supremacy of the U.S. Constitution, state constitutions, and legislation adopted by Congress and state legislatures. Thus, the common law is both a flexible legal code and an instrument of judicial lawmaking.

Federal and State Law

The Constitution confers on Congress various specifications of authority, including comprehensive authority to regulate commerce with foreign countries and "among the several states." The national government's authority over commerce includes authority to create legal obligations and relationships between private parties in matters affecting business, finance, and industry. It is exercised through congressional legislation, which prescribes the principal provisions and typically authorizes supplemental and more detailed regulations to be promulgated by an agency charged with administering the statute. Over time, the statutes and regulations are further explicated through judicial decisions. However, the primary medium of federal law remains that of statute, both new legislative measures and occasional amendment of long-standing statutes.

Such a body of federal law regulates, for example, the minimum wage and working conditions of employees in industry; equal treatment of employees with regard to race, gender, and age; rights and obligations in the securities markets and banking relationships; business transactions involving fraud; responsibilities for preserving the environment; and many of the rights of travelers and shippers by air, rail, and highway transportation.

Legal obligations created by federal statute often provide that the obligations may be enforced through litigation between private parties. For example, the laws regulating the sale of corporate shares of stock provide that participants in such transactions may enforce violations through suit against a violator. So also a person suffering discrimination in employment or from violation of federal safety regulations may sue for personal injury damages. The authority to prosecute such a suit is called a private right of action; this enforcement mechanism coexists with the authority of governmental administrative agencies to seek penal sanctions for violation. Accordingly, much of federal public law may be enforced through private-party actions for damages or injunctive relief in the courts. This kind of litigation constitutes a major part of the activity of the federal courts.

Although the federal government is supreme in matters within its sphere, historically and conceptually the states are the primary organic government. As explained above, the states existed before the United States and were legally autonomous sovereigns in the period after the Revolution. Each state that has since been added to the union stands in that same constitutional relationship to the national federation. Thus, each of the original states had a complete structure of government and a complete legal system upon joining the federation, and so has each state created since.

The relationship between federal law and state law can be summarized schematically as follows: state law governs all legal relationships between private parties except where federal law has been enacted on a subject, in which event federal law is authoritative. However, federal law usually takes the form of specific provisions dealing with limited legal aspects of a social relationship, rather than a comprehensive federal code defining all aspects of a relationship. For example, in an employment relationship in industry, federal law prescribes the minimum wage that must be paid and requires equal treatment of employees regardless of race, gender, and age, but state law regulates the compensation paid for injury suffered in the course of employment and governs the parties' rights and duties upon termination of the employment relationship. For further example, in transactions concerning securities such as stocks and bonds, federal law governs the disclosures of fact that a seller of securities must make, but state law determines when ownership of a security has been transferred and the rights of succession to ownership upon the death of the original owner.

The relationship between federal and state law can present intricate technical questions that must be resolved in adjudication of controversies involving both state and federal law.

The Federal Court System

The U.S. Constitution makes provision for the federal court system in Article III, which states: "The judicial Power of the United States, shall be vested in one supreme Court, and in such inferior Courts as the Congress may from time to time ordain and establish." Article III contemplated that Congress by statute should specify the composition of the Supreme Court and should establish a system of subordinate courts. Immediately after the adoption of the Constitution, Congress adopted the Judiciary Act of 1789. That act constituted the Supreme Court with seven justices to sit at the seat of government; created a lower court system consisting of a district court in each state to exercise trial jurisdiction and circuit courts in which two judges would sit as a trial court in important cases; and made provision for procedure in the various courts. Over the years alterations have continually been made to this structure: for example, enlarging the Supreme Court to nine members, dividing district courts in the more populous states into several judicial districts, and transforming the circuits into a level of intermediate appellate courts. However, the federal court system as it exists today is the direct descendant of the original establishment.

The federal court system now consists of a pyramid of authority, with the U.S. Supreme Court at the apex, the U.S. courts of appeals at the intermediate level, and the U.S. district courts at the base.

The district courts are trial courts or, in comparative law terminology, tribunals of the first instance. They have competence to adjudicate all matters within the authority of the federal court system, with very few exceptions. Cases within the district courts' competence include both civil and criminal matters, for federal law not only creates civil obligations but also prescribes many kinds of criminal offenses.

District courts are established throughout the country and are organized along the territorial boundaries of the states. Each state consists of at least one district and the larger states have several districts. For example, the state of New York has four territorial districts, while the state of New Jersey consists of one district. The U.S. territories, including the Virgin Islands and Guam, and the Commonwealth of Puerto Rico each also have a federal district court.

The Constitution provides that the federal courts may have jurisdiction of several types of cases:

Those arising under federal law, whether the Constitution, statute, or treaties. This provision enables federal law to be enforced in federal as well as in state court.

Those in which the United States is a party. This provision enables the federal government to have recourse to the federal courts in matters involving the government itself.

Those in which the litigants are citizens of different states. This provision was designed to reduce the risk that out-of-state litigants will suffer prejudicial treatment in state courts.

Admiralty cases. Litigation arising from maritime commerce was especially important in the early days of the Republic.

Cases involving foreign citizens and governments. Litigation involving foreigners often involves sensitive matters of international relations.

The Constitution contemplated that these jurisdictional provisions be implemented by congressional legislation. Congress has granted the district courts jurisdiction under all of the specifications outlined above, although not to the full extent that would be possible under the Constitution. For example, the statutes permit claims based on federal law to be brought in federal court but not cases in which federal law is a basis of the defendant's defense. Hence, in determining a federal court's jurisdiction it is necessary to refer to statutory provisions as well as to the Constitution.

Each district court has several judges, the number being provided by statute and adjusted over the years. Today almost every district has at least five judges and some have as many as twenty. One of the judges of each district, selected on the basis of seniority, is chief judge. The chief judge is responsible for the general administration of the court but has no greater judicial authority than the other judges. Cases are usually assigned to specific judges by a random procedure and each judge is responsible individually for cases assigned to him or her. All judicial matters are considered and determined by a single judge. This procedure contrasts with that in most other countries, where all but very minor cases are adjudicated before a three-person tribunal. The only exception to this rule in the federal courts is a procedure for a three-judge panel in very limited circumstances involving the constitutionality of certain election reapportionment laws.

The U.S. courts of appeals, as their name implies, have appellate jurisdiction. In comparative law terminology, such courts are called second-instance tribunals. The courts of appeals are primarily organized on a geographical basis, in territories called circuits. (The term *circuit* derives from the fact that in the early days of the federal court system, judges traveled from one district to another in an itinerary called a circuit.) The basis of this territorial organization is the boundaries of the states. For example, the U.S. Court of Appeals for the Third Circuit consists of the states of New Jersey, Pennsylvania, and Delaware, together with the territory of the Virgin Islands. There are twelve such territorial circuits, including one for the District of Columbia, the seat of the federal government in Washington. There are also two courts of appeals with specialized jurisdiction and national territorial scope: the Court of Appeals for the Federal Circuit, which has jurisdiction of patent, trademark, and certain other cases, and the Court of Claims, which has jurisdiction of various kinds of cases against the government.

Each court of appeals has several judges, the number being provided by statute and adjusted over the years. Some circuits have fewer than ten judges and one has more than twenty-five. Each circuit has a chief judge who is responsible for general administration of the court but has no greater judicial authority than the other judges. Appeals in the courts of appeals usually are considered by panels of three judges, who are assigned to specific cases by a random selection procedure. In cases of exceptional importance, all the judges of the circuit may hear and decide the matter, a procedure called an *en banc* hearing. En banc hearings may be held to determine constitutional issues or cases in which panels of the court have reached inconsistent results.

The courts of appeals have appellate jurisdiction over all appeals from the U.S. district courts, with few exceptions. In very limited circumstances, involving questions of extraordinary urgency, an appeal may proceed from a federal district court directly to the Supreme Court. This occurred in 1974 in *United States v. Nixon,* the "Watergate" case involving the President's obligation to respond to an order of the court.[6] The courts of appeals have no appellate jurisdiction over matters in the state courts.

The Supreme Court of the United States consists of nine justices, including the Chief Justice. The Chief Justice presides in the Supreme Court and has general supervisory responsibility for the federal court system as a whole. However, the Chief Justice has no greater judicial authority than the other justices. The Supreme Court sits as a group in all matters, except when a justice does not participate because of illness or for some other special reason.

The Supreme Court has appellate jurisdiction over the U.S. courts of appeal. It also has jurisdiction of appeals from the state courts with respect to questions of federal law. A case in the state courts involving the interpretation of the U.S. Constitution, or of a federal statute or treaty, therefore may be appealed to the Supreme Court. The Supreme Court's appellate jurisdiction over the state court is vital constitutionally and important for the legal system. However, it is exercised in no more than a few dozen of the full decisions the Supreme Court undertakes each year.

The Supreme Court receives thousands of applications for appeal each year, most of them called "petitions for certiorari." Such a petition briefly describes the case and the legal issues it presents and asks the court to accept the case among those that it will consider in its forthcoming session. Once a week the Court has a "cert. conference," a closed session in which the justices consider these petitions. Most of the applications are rejected. The power to grant or deny certiorari is within the Court's complete discretion and may be exercised without public explanation; when a petition is denied, an order is simply entered. About 120 to 150 cases per year are accepted for full consideration. The Court takes some judicial action in several hundred additional cases, for example, reversing the lower court decision with directions that the case be reconsidered in light of some decision that has been recently issued by the Court. Most of the Supreme Court's cases directly or implicitly involve questions of procedural law.

State Court Systems

Every state has its own court system based upon its own constitution. Most state constitutions prescribe the composition and jurisdiction of the courts, so that the state legislatures have only limited authority to make legislative provisions concerning the courts. An illustrative state constitutional provision is that in California: "The Judicial power of this State is vested in the Supreme Court, courts of appeal, superior courts and justice courts."[7]

The court systems of the original thirteen states were created before the formation of the federal union, having been constituted by charter or ordinance from the English government in colonial times. Following the Revolution, the states reestablished these courts by constitutional provision that incorporated the courts' previous authority. The states created after formation of the federal union in 1789 have constitutions with generally similar provisions.

The structures of the state court systems are generally similar to the federal court system. The state courts of first instance are referred to as "trial courts of general jurisdiction," signifying that their competence includes all criminal and civil matters except those assigned to other specialized tribunals. Their competence includes cases involving federal law except in limited categories of cases, for example, suits under the Sherman Antitrust Act, for which a federal statute provides that the jurisdiction of the federal courts is exclusive. Accordingly, the trial courts of the states may be regarded as the foundational tribunals in the American legal system. Many states have a subordinate level of trial courts for determining minor civil disputes and the preliminary stage of criminal prosecutions.

The title of the trial court varies from state to state—for example, "superior court," "district court," or "county court." In each state the trial courts are organized on a territorial basis according to county boundaries. For example, in California there is a Superior Court for Los Angeles County, one for San Francisco, and one for each of the other counties in the state. Each such court has at least one judge. Rural counties ordinarily have a single judge; large metropolitan trial courts have dozens of judges. Each court has a presiding judge responsible for the court's administration. As in the federal court system, all trial judges are of equal authority and in adjudication function individually and not in multijudge panels.

The trial courts of a state system handle many more cases than the federal district courts in the same state. In fact, new cases are filed in the state courts many times as frequently as in the federal district courts, the rate varying from state to state. For example, statistics from 1989 indicate that federal district courts had four hundred new civil cases and one hundred serious (felony) criminal cases per judge, while some state judges in the same year had nearly twenty-five hundred new cases.[8] It must be recognized that the complexity of the average federal case, civil or criminal, is greater than that in state court. Nevertheless, the statistics demonstrate how large a portion of the administration of civil justice is carried out by the state courts. In 1989, the state courts received 17.3 million new civil cases, plus additional millions of criminal, domestic, and traffic cases, while the federal trial courts received approximately 235,000 civil cases. The state court systems thus have about seventy times as many cases as the federal court system.

In quantitative terms as well, the state trial courts are the foundational tribunals of the American legal system.

Most states have a level of second-instance courts called intermediate appellate courts, similar to the courts of appeals in the federal system. The title of the intermediate appellate court is usually "court of appeals." These courts have many judges, in some states as many as fifty or more, but they function in panels of three, as in the federal appellate system. Their competence includes all proceedings originally adjudicated in the state trial courts, with very limited exceptions. They have no appellate authority with regard to the federal district courts or courts of appeal. The decisions of a state's intermediate appellate court are subject to further appeal to the state's highest court. The state intermediate appellate courts taken as a whole decide thousands of cases each year, most of them supported by written opinions.

Each state has a supreme court with competency of appeals from the lower courts in the system. Appeal to the state supreme court from lower courts usually requires the supreme court's permission. The state supreme court is the final authority in interpreting the law of that state. However, decisions by a state supreme court concerning matters of federal law are subject to further appeal to the U.S. Supreme Court.

In most states the supreme court consists of seven judges, who usually function en banc, not in panels. The chief justice, usually selected on the basis of seniority or appointed by the governor, presides over the court and has general supervisory responsibility for the court system as a whole. The typical state supreme court decides between one hundred and three hundred cases per year, in addition to determining petitions seeking permission to bring an appeal.

The accompanying diagram shows the structure of the federal court system on the left and of a typical state court system on the right.

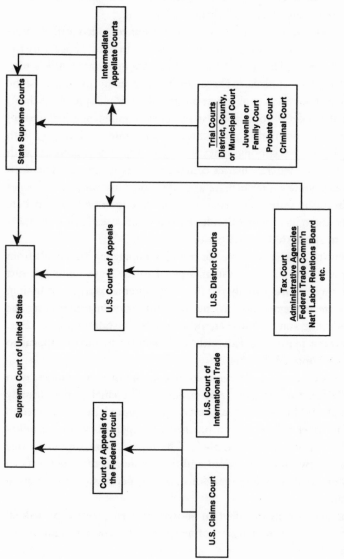

The structure of the American court system. From *Want's Federal-State Court Directory.* Copyright 1991 by WANT Publishing Co. Reprinted by permission.

CHAPTER THREE

The Authority and Functions of American Courts

The most distinctive characteristic of the courts in the United States is their involvement in determining issues that in other countries are determined outside the courts. Fundamental issues in which the American courts have been instrumental include racial desegregation, abortion, rights of the accused in criminal cases, freedom of speech, and the relationship between religion and the government. In all other modern democracies these issues have been treated almost exclusively as "political" matters. That is, they have been determined by parliamentary legislation, or by the decision of a cabinet composed of parliamentary leaders, or by decisions of the permanent government bureaucracy with which the parliamentary leadership decided not to interfere. The same is true of many issues having lower public visibility but great significance in the world of business and commercial transactions.

The role of the courts in resolving "political" issues has been a central phenomenon of American government since the adoption of the Constitution. The supporters of the Constitution anticipated that the federal court system would restrain the excesses of "faction," by which the Federalists meant popular sentiment. In recent years the role of the courts has been intensely debated in connection with appointments to the U.S. Supreme Court, for example, those of Robert Bork (who was rejected) and of Clarence Thomas (who was confirmed).

The idea that the courts, a nonelective agency of government, can decide fundamental political issues contradicts all conventional theories of democracy. Yet the courts of the United States, the world's longest-established constitutional democracy, perform that very function. The paradox of nondemocratic authority being central in a constitutional democracy has defied political theorists since Tocqueville focused attention on it over 150 years ago. A coherent explanation, if there is one, must be complex. Some insight can be gained by reflecting on the fact that the vehicle for this exercise of judicial authority is ordinary litigation and not some special constitutional process.

Ordinary litigation is available to anyone, at least anyone who can find a lawyer willing to take the case. Entry into the American legal profession has been very open since colonial days, and there have always been plenty of lawyers. Hence, almost anyone with a good legal cause can find means to bring it. This right of political access expresses principles of equality and opportunity that are fundamental in American consciousness.

Ordinary litigation calls upon protection of the law, not an exercise of discretion or grace by a government official. Of course, judges in fact are government officials and have broad discretion in all their decisions. In concept, however, the judges merely give voice to legal rights, and in concept those rights are universally shared in a community itself constituted by a legal instrument—the Constitution. A lawsuit, particularly as conducted through the adversary system, is an expression of legal equality, a principle fundamental in American consciousness.

Ordinary litigation summons a citizen, even one having wealth or power, to account for his or her conduct in specific terms and humbling circumstances. The defendant must answer the charges, produce documents from otherwise confidential files, and respond to cross-examination. Judgment is passed by judges who are more or less politically independent and juries comprised of people from everyday walks of life. This too expresses basic political principles.

Ordinary litigation is conducted in tribunals that deal with the whole range of civil life. On any given day the courts may determine rights between neighbors concerning the use of a driveway; employees and employers over the rights of labor and management; police and criminal suspects over the rules governing arrest; divorcing spouses; consumers and sellers; manufacturers and distributors; rival political candidates; motorists; debtors and creditors; government and taxpayers; and government and the governed. In any given judgment, the courts will have mediated between almost every set of social, economic, and political interests, all in the name of legal justice. The courts represent an institutional version of Plato's ideal philosopher-king, or perhaps the biblical ideal personified in Solomon as king-judge. These images are the products of a strong sense that politics have a moral foundation.

Constitutional Law

In formal terms, the legal powers of the courts include interpreting the written constitutions that are the foundations of the federal and state governments; redefining the common law, which is the primary source of private law; and interpreting legislation, which is democracy's primary medium of policy choice. In addition, the courts have important authority to review and control the activities of administrative agencies.

The U.S. Constitution and the constitutions of the states are the legal source of all government authority. As we have seen in chapter 2, the Constitution establishes the federal government and its three branches, prescribes the authority of Congress to legislate in matters of national concern, and imposes legal requirements on the manner in which government's authority is exercised. The Constitution includes important provisions for the protection of individual rights—notably the Due Process Clause, the right to assistance of legal counsel in criminal matters prescribed in the Sixth Amendment, and a prohibition on government taking private property without just compensation.

Every clause and every word of the Constitution has potential legal significance. Constitutional provisions confer protections on individuals that may be invoked by individuals in ordinary litigation concerning their interests. Many of the constitutional provisions defining the powers of the legislative and executive branches of government may also be drawn into consideration in ordinary judicial proceedings. Hence, virtually every provision of the Constitution has been the subject of litigation and, as a consequence, of judicial decisions. Taken together these decisions, along with scholarly and professional commentary, have created a set of authoritative pronouncements called "constitutional law."

In common usage, the term *constitutional law* refers to the U.S. Constitution and the decisional law interpreting that document. However, each state has a constitution that occupies a corresponding position for that state's government. State constitutional provisions may be invoked in ordinary civil litigation, just as the counterpart provisions of the U.S. Constitution may be. A party to a civil dispute sometimes will rely on both the U.S. Constitution and the constitution of the specific state. In a more general sense, therefore, constitutional law includes the textual interpretation of state constitutions as well as of the U.S. Constitution.

The U.S. Supreme Court has ultimate legal authority to interpret the Constitution. As stated in the classic decision in *Marbury v. Madison,* "it is emphatically the province of the judiciary to say what the law is."[1] The supreme courts of the states have equivalent authority to interpret state constitutions, subject to the supremacy of the federal Constitution. The authority of the judiciary in constitutional interpretation includes the power to declare legislation unconstitutional. This power, called "judicial review," gives the courts legal authority superior to that of the legislature.

It is important to recognize that the authority to interpret and apply constitutional law reposes in all courts of first instance and all appellate courts. This authority must be exercised whenever a party properly relies on a constitutional provision in the course of ordinary civil litigation. Constitutional law is therefore merely an aspect of the law applied by all courts in all ordinary litigation. When a statute is found to be unconstitutional by the courts, the courts simply refuse to apply the statute. The statute technically remains in force as the official act of the legislature, but the court's decision is a precedent that bars it from being applied by the judiciary. Theoretically, if the court later reversed itself on the constitutional issue, the statue could thereafter be validly applied. In practice, when the legislature wishes to reassert the constitutional issue, it does so by enacting a new statute, which then may be the subject of new constitutional litigation.

Reformation of the Common Law

As explained in chapters 1 and 2, the common law was both a system of civil procedure and a body of substantive law. Originally, its principles dealt primarily with rights in land arising from feudal relationships. Over the years, the common law came to govern personal property, contractual obligations, and civil wrongs such as fraud and injury to the person. By the time of the European settlement in North America, the common law had evolved to a broad legal framework. Carried forward ever since, the common law is the basis for judicial decisions in matters not governed by statute. Hence, decisional law is authoritative except as superseded by legislation or constitutional provisions.

At any given time, decisional law can be considered as definite and fixed, and in this form can be stated as a comprehensive legal code. Legal scholars in various fields of law expound and comment on the common law in these terms. For example, there are treatises on contract law, property law, and all other legal subjects, reflecting the accumulated decisional law. However, it is also recognized that the common law is changed through decisions over time. Every area of American law provides classic examples of the remaking of common law rules. For instance, the law of misrepresentation in contract negotiations changed from "buyer beware" to "seller be forthright"; the law governing personal injury expanded from compensation for causing physical injury to compensation for causing emotional distress; and defamation originally could be based on making statements that were true, but in the present era liability has come to be limited, in the case of statements about public officials, to statements known to be false or made without serious investigation into their truth. Much of the study and understanding of the common law consists of historical analysis of such changes. Thus, while decisional law remains constant from one point of view, in broader perspective it can be seen to be changing continuously.

The common law is primarily private law and generally does not address such subjects as the regulation of business and the powers of government. However, many common law principles indirectly affect the legal powers of government. Principles of fairness in the law governing private relations influence the interpretation of legislation and the review of administrative authority. For example, once it has been established that the seller in a private contractual relationship must be open and forthright with a buyer, it seems logical to apply this principle to dealings between a government agency and a citizen. Moreover, the courts' long-established authority to pronounce common law strongly influences the attitude of American judges in their interpretation of constitutions and legislation. Judges refer not only to the text of a constitutional or legislative provision but also to their own prior decisions interpreting the text. Over time, the interpretive decisions become a substantial body of law in themselves. This kind of displacement is contrary to the basic theory of other modern legal systems.

Statutory Interpretation

The interpretation of legislation is approached in a frame of mind shaped by the courts' authority in constitutional law and common law.[2] For example, legislation dealing with individual rights or with governmental agency procedure is interpreted in terms of the courts' decisional law on these subjects. If parties in court are entitled to see documents in the possession of the other side, it seems logical to apply this principle to proceedings conducted by government agencies. Another illustration is the judiciary's approach to commercial law. Commercial law is now codified in statute, but the commercial codes do not exhaustively cover all types of transactions. Hence, the judiciary brings to the interpretation of commercial code legislation its own historically derived legal concepts and its familiarity with the common law rules governing similar transactions.

The judicial viewpoint is also expressed in the interpretation of textually vague legislation. Congress and the state legislatures often adopt statutory provisions containing very broad and uncertain language. The legislatures foresee and expect that the courts will supply detail through interpretation. This kind of delegation to the courts often allows the legislature to avoid making controversial choices among conflicting social interests. However, delegating interpretative detail to the courts is also a recognition that the courts' practice of making such decisions has been legitimated by tradition.

As a consequence, the significance of many statutes lies less in the language of the statute than in the judicial precedents interpreting the statute. An example is the Sherman Antitrust Act, enacted in 1890, which prohibits business agreements that restrain competition. The Sherman Act is cast in very general language. Over the course of a century, it has been interpreted in hundreds of judicial decisions concerning a wide variety of business arrangements in dozens of different industries, businesses, and professions. These interpretations constitute a complex body of law whose content is primarily the decisions themselves rather than the language of the act. The same is true of many other areas of the law in which the foundation is a statute but the critical detail is in the accumulation of interpretative judicial decisions.

With respect to legislation dealing with subject matter outside the judiciary's domain, however, the courts are much more deferential to the legislature's objectives and the language of the statute. This attitude is exhibited in matters of taxation, for example, where the courts recognize the legislature's broad authority to determine what activities are to be taxed and the formulae and rates of taxation. Hence, taxation statutes tend to be interpreted and applied in a technical and literalistic fashion. Nevertheless, it is noteworthy that the function of interpreting and applying such legislation has been performed primarily by the general court system, and not through a special system of tax courts.

Review of Administrative Agencies

There are myriad administrative agencies in American government—the "bureaucracies" that citizens, the media, and politicians chronically complain about. These agencies perform all kinds of functions at all levels of government. They manage public education and public transportation; regulate all kinds of financial, business, and consumer transactions; supervise licensed professions and vocations; and so forth.

The authority of the courts over administrative agencies derives from three fundamental legal principles. First, an administrative agency must confine its action to that authorized by statute. There is no general principle of "state necessity," as there is in some other legal systems, that empowers agencies to undertake activities not authorized by statute. In determining the scope of administrative agency powers, therefore, the courts have final authority to interpret the statutes that confer such powers.

Second, an administrative agency generally must exercise its powers according to the procedures prescribed in general statutes governing administrative agency procedure. A federal statute known as the Administrative Procedure Act prescribes such procedures for federal agencies, and most states have similar statutes governing procedure of their agencies. In addition, an agency must conform to special statutory procedures applicable to the specific agency. The courts have final authority to determine what procedures are required by the governing statutes.

Third, a general principle of due process prohibits an agency from acting in "arbitrary or capricious" fashion. Although this broad principle is applied only in extreme cases of administrative irregularity, it is a residual basis for judicial scrutiny of the legal propriety of administrative agency actions.

These legal principles, and corollaries to them, can be applied by the ordinary courts in suits brought at the instance of private parties. An example is *Brown v. Board of Education,* the famous case that invalidated racial segregation in public schools. In terms of the competence of the courts and the form of proceedings, this was a challenge to administrative action on the part of a governmental agency. The plaintiffs in *Brown* were parents of children enrolled in schools in Topeka, Kansas. The administrative action of which they complained was the school district's rule that black children could not enroll in schools with white children. The complaint was in the form employed in ordinary civil procedure and was brought in the court of first instance in Kansas. The remedy sought was an injunction to prevent the school board from giving effect to its segregation rules. The legal argument in support of the complaint was that the segregation of black students denied them equal protection of the law. This argument was pursued through appeal to the U.S. Supreme Court, which sustained it.

Many administrative agencies have tribunals as part of their internal structure. Thus, an agency having powers of regulation, investigation, and supervision may also have a system of tribunals for adjudicating disputes between the agency and private persons who are subject to its regulatory authority. These tribunals have presiding officers called administrative law judges. They receive evidence in testimonial and documentary form, and they consider and resolve legal arguments. Typically, the case on behalf of the agency is presented by an agency prosecutor. In cases involving substantial stakes, the private parties involved are represented by counsel. There are established rules of procedure and regularized customs of practice. For all practical purposes, these tribunals are courts.

However, in legal principle they are not courts in the full constitutional sense. Instead, they are considered independent or executive agencies. As such, their decisions are subject to challenge in the ordinary civil courts. The proceedings for such challenges are generically known as judicial review of administrative agency action. Judicial review often takes the form of a civil lawsuit against the head of the administrative agency, in which the grievance is the alleged failure of the agency to have conducted itself according to law.

A judicial review proceeding generally is based on the record of the proceedings before the administrative tribunal. Hence, the court in the civil review proceeding does not receive new evidence. Rather, its function concerning factual issues is limited to determining whether the administrative tribunal's conclusion was reasonably supported by evidence. On the other hand, issues of law are open for fresh consideration by the court. Thus, if the court determines that the administrative tribunal misinterpreted the applicable statute concerning its powers or the merits of the controversy, the court interposes its own interpretation and renders judgment accordingly.

Some judicial review proceedings are conducted before ordinary courts of the first instance, others before the intermediate appellate courts. The question of competence in this respect is determined by no general principle but by the statute governing the specific agency. If no provision is made in a statute governing an administrative agency, then judicial review may be obtained through a suit for an injunction or similar remedy in a court of first instance. The suit is brought against the agency official; the relief sought is that the official be ordered to act in accordance with law as determined by the court. Appellate review of judicial review proceedings generally follows the same channels as appeals in ordinary civil litigation. Thus, a judicial review proceeding commenced in the state court of first instance may then be appealed to the state intermediate appellate court and thereafter to the state supreme court. A parallel channel is followed in judicial review proceedings in the federal court system. State courts have no authority to review determinations of federal administrative agencies. However, federal district courts in certain circumstances have authority to review determinations of state administrative agencies. This authority may be exercised when the state administrative agency is acting in a manner that violates federal constitutional law or federal legislation governing the state function.

Opportunity for judicial review is a constitutional right. The constitutional concept is that without such opportunity, the affected private party will have suffered deprivation without due process of law. That is, legal due process in adjudication of personal rights can be rendered only in a court or in an administrative tribunal whose determinations are subject to judicial review.

The American judiciary is thus empowered to give authoritative interpretation to the U.S. Constitution and the state constitutions and to rely on their own precedents concerning such interpretation; to interpret legislation by similar technique; to apply their own decisional law in the absence of constitutional or legislative provisions; to pronounce through decision the legal rule to be applied in novel matters not governed by legislation; and to review the legal regularity of actions of governmental agencies. Taken together, these are substantial lawmaking functions.

Criminal Justice

The ordinary courts have competence over criminal prosecutions as well as over civil litigation. There are federal crimes, proscribed by federal statute, and crimes proscribed by state law. In general, conduct defined as a federal crime is related in one way or another to functions of the federal government. Thus, it is a federal crime to assault or commit homicide against various federal officials, including the President of the United States. It is a federal crime to use the mail service (which is provided under the aegis of the federal government) to commit fraud. Various kinds of business and securities offenses are also made criminal by federal law.

However, federal criminal law, like federal civil law, is in principle exceptional. Basic penal law is established by state legislation, including the law of homicide, rape, kidnapping, assault, theft, and criminal fraud. Both state and federal laws prohibit use or sale of drugs such as cocaine and marijuana.

State criminal law is enforced by police whose authority is derived from state law, including municipal police, county sheriffs departments, and state police. Federal criminal law is enforced by such agencies as the Federal Bureau of Investigation, the Postal Inspector's Office, and various regulatory agencies. The taxing authorities of the federal and state governments have their own investigative authorities.

Federal crimes are prosecuted in federal court by federal prosecuting attorneys. The U.S. district courts are the first-instance federal courts in criminal matters, as is in civil matters. Appeals in criminal cases are within the competence of the circuit courts of appeal, by procedure similar to that in civil appeals.

Each district court has a U.S. attorney, appointed by the President and assisted by a staff of other lawyers and office assistants. The staff are generally selected on the basis of professional merit and many serve on a career basis. The U.S. attorneys are subject to general supervision by the attorney general of the United States, who is the head of the Department of Justice. First-instance criminal proceedings in federal court are handled by the local U.S. attorney's office. Appeals are handled by the Department of Justice, headquartered in Washington, D.C. Persons convicted of federal crimes are under federal penal supervision and, if sentenced to prison, are incarcerated in federal prisons.

State crimes are prosecuted in state court by state prosecuting attorneys. In most states the court having first-instance civil competence also has first-instance criminal competence. However, in a few states there are separate criminal trial courts. In almost all states, appeals in state criminal cases proceed to the intermediate courts of appeal, which also have competence over civil appeals, although a few states have separate courts of criminal appeal. In almost all states, the state supreme court has competence of further appeals from the intermediate courts of appeal. Such appeals to the state supreme court in criminal cases are usually discretionary with the supreme court, similar to discretionary appeal in civil cases. However, in states having capital punishment, a sentence of death is usually appealable of right to the state supreme court.

Prosecution of state criminal cases is conducted by state prosecuting attorneys, known as "district attorneys" or "state's attorneys." The offices of prosecuting attorneys are usually organized along county lines, the same territorial basis for the courts of first instance. In most states each county's prosecuting attorney is chosen by local popular election, but in a few states the office is appointive. The prosecutor's office has a supporting staff, which in large urban communities can include dozens or hundreds of lawyers and corresponding numbers of office personnel. These staffs usually have at least ordinary legal competence, but political affiliations are significant in many localities. The vast bulk of criminal prosecutions occur in state courts.

The procedure in criminal prosecutions in federal courts is prescribed by constitutional provisions, federal legislation, and federal rules of court. The procedure in criminal prosecutions in state courts is generally prescribed by counterpart state procedure. However, criminal procedure in state courts is subject to many requirements imposed through the Due Process and Equal Protection clauses of the U.S. Constitution. For example, federal constitutional law requires that proof in a criminal case be established "beyond a reasonable doubt." Constitutional law also requires the right of jury trial in serious crimes and requires that in such prosecutions an indigent defendant be provided with legal counsel at public expense.

Because constitutional law imposes many requirements on prosecution of crimes in state courts, issues of federal law frequently arise in state criminal cases. These issues, after having been reviewed in the state appellate system, are subject to appeal before the U.S. Supreme Court. Thus, the Supreme Court has final authority over federal legal questions arising not only in criminal prosecutions, civil cases in lower federal courts, and civil cases in the state courts, but also in state criminal prosecutions.

Political Appointment of Judges

The fact that the American judiciary exercises substantial lawmaking authority helps explain the strongly political nature of the process of selecting judges. In most modern countries the judiciary is regarded as politically inert and its membership appointed by a correspondingly nonpolitical process. In most European and Latin American countries and in Japan, judicial office is a career that begins immediately after completion of legal education. Graduates aspiring to the judiciary must pass special examinations and complete special judicial training; they then enter the judicial ranks as assistant judges in the lowest courts. Advancement proceeds by seniority and upon evaluation by superiors within the judiciary. Judges at all levels are the products of this meritocratic system.

The methods of judicial selection in the United States are quite different and distinctly political. Federal judges are nominated by the President and must be confirmed by a two-thirds vote of the Senate. This procedure applies to justices of the Supreme Court and to judges of the lower federal courts. Legally, the President may nominate anyone, without regard to professional qualifications. In practice, nominees are lawyers who have had substantial experience in public or private law practice, rarely less than ten years. For the Supreme Court, the established practice is that the nominee must have extensive experience as a judge, public administrator, or lawyer, and be professionally recognized as competent.

The political controls on appointment and promotion of judges operate as an important constraint on the judiciary's autonomy. For many years the pretense was maintained that a nominee for the Supreme Court should be considered only in terms of professional qualifications. However, from the very early years political considerations weighed heavily in these appointments and in those to the lower federal courts. For example, John Marshall was appointed Chief Justice by the Federalist President John Adams in 1801 in anticipation of the incoming Democratic President Thomas Jefferson; judicial appointments by President Franklin Roosevelt in the

1930s were designed to change the Supreme Court's attitude toward New Deal legislation. Until recent years, however, political factors were not openly acknowledged.

The President's nomination for a federal judgeship is submitted to the Senate, where the Judiciary Committee inquires into the nominee's qualifications. The committee makes a recommendation to the Senate either for or against the appointment. The nomination is then voted upon by the Senate as a whole. As dramatically illustrated by the nomination of Robert Bork, the process of confirmation can be highly partisan and controversial.[3] However, once appointed, a federal judge retains office for life, subject only to removal by impeachment for serious misconduct. No Supreme Court justice has ever been removed from office. Impeachment of lower federal court judges has been rare and only for criminal misconduct such as bribery. For all practical purposes, federal judges have lifetime appointments.

Appointment of judges to the federal courts of appeals and district courts is governed by considerations similar to those influencing appointments to the Supreme Court. By tradition, district judges are chosen from among judges and lawyers residing in the district to which the appointment is made. Thus, judges of the U.S. District Court for Ohio have been Ohio judges or lawyers. A similar tradition generally applies to the court of appeals. Very often judges of state courts are appointed to positions in the federal judiciary, and such an appointment is regarded as a professional promotion. By tradition, the Senate influences the nomination of lower federal court judges as well as their confirmation. Senators who are of the same party as the President make recommendations of circuit and district judges, which the President ordinarily treats as decisive.

Promotion to a higher level within the federal court system is accomplished by the same process. Thus, a district judge may become a circuit judge only upon nomination by the President and confirmation by the Senate; the judiciary has no authority to make internal promotions. As a result, many of the judges recognized as most able may remain in the lower courts, while politically more acceptable nominees gain promotion.

The relationship between political considerations and professional qualifications in the appointment of judges is complex and subtle. Only on rare occasions does a prospective appointment become the subject of general public attention or debate. Furthermore, since federal judges, once appointed, have permanent tenure "upon good behavior," it is virtually impossible to organize a successful campaign to force a judge out of office. In 1970, an effort was made to impeach Supreme Court Justice William O. Douglas, but it rapidly failed.

Instead, political influence is exerted in the selection of new appointees. Political influence usually is brought to bear through "corridor" politics—discussions among influential political leaders concerning prospective appointments and promotions. Sometimes popular sentiment plays a direct part through organized protest campaigns.

The political controls exercised through the process of nomination by the President and confirmation by the Senate, while informal and indirect, have pervasive influence on the federal judiciary. Federal judges, even though they are not directly accountable politically, are intensely aware of political factors in administering the law. However, there is no assurance that a person once appointed will fulfill the political expectations suggested by the nominee's background. A notable instance was Chief Justice Earl Warren, a moderate Republican governor of California who became a strong activist as Chief Justice, particularly in the fields of race relations and criminal justice.

The procedures for selection of state judges vary widely but also strongly reflect political considerations. A continuing fundamental issue in many states is the method of selecting judges. In general, the question is whether judges should be elected, thus giving direct effect to popular sentiment, or appointed, thus allowing more careful scrutiny of a candidate's qualifications.

In many states, trial judges are elected by popular vote. Various special election procedures for judges have been devised to reduce the effects of direct electoral politics. In some states, for example, a trial judge is appointed by the governor and then must submit to a plebiscite without an opposing candidate. In many states, opposition candidates are permitted but the judicial election proceeds without party designation of the candidates. In most states appellate judges are appointed by the governor, subject to confirmation by either the legislature or a judicial qualifications commission. In practice, an appointee to an appellate court ordinarily must have substantial experience as a judge of a lower court and at least some acquaintance in politics.

In most states a judicial appointment is for a fixed term, typically six or eight years. At the end of their terms, state court judges whose office is elective are subject to reelection or defeat; a judge whose office is by appointment is subject to a reappointment procedure. In most states judges are usually reelected or reappointed unless they have been guilty of misbehavior or have excited broad public hostility by their decisions. However, the degree of judicial responsiveness to political influence varies widely among the various states, and also varies somewhat according to the judge's position in the judicial hierarchy. In New Jersey, for example, the system for appointing judges is similar to that in the federal courts. Judges in that state are appointed by the governor subject to confirmation by the state senate, and serve with expectation of reappointment even if their decisions have been controversial. In contrast, judges in some other states are chosen by popular elections with party affiliation and must face election campaigns at the end of terms as short as four years. Trial judges in such a system are highly sensitive to local political issues, such as controversial crimes, and judges of appellate courts are highly sensitive to issues such as taxation and regulation of business. In most states judicial office is therefore somewhat insecure and judges handle politically sensitive cases with caution.

From a comparative perspective, American judges are distinctive in several respects: their professional backgrounds include law practice, primarily in private firms and in public prosecutor's offices; they are appointed by political authorities who give consideration to political factors; eligibility as a practical matter usually requires experience in politics; promotion within the judicial system is in the hands of the political branches; and, except in the federal court system and a few of the states, their tenure is subject to some political jeopardy.

In terms of professional qualifications, the range of competence among American judges is very wide. In the federal court system and the systems of such states as California and New Jersey, the judges in general are very capable compared with practicing lawyers and other professionals. In some state courts, however, judges can be elected whose only qualifications are that they have been admitted to practice law and that their names are familiar to the electorate, for example, because of family involvement in politics. Comparisons of professional qualifications are difficult to make, certainly from one country to another. Nevertheless, it is fair to say that on average the professional ability of American judges is no less than that in other legal systems, but also that the variation among American judges is very wide.

The Unique Position of the Supreme Court

The U.S. Supreme Court has a position of authority unlike that of any other judicial tribunal in the world.

The Supreme Court is, first of all, the highest authority in the federal court system. As we have seen, the federal court system has exclusive competence over criminal proceedings for enforcing federal criminal law. In the modern era, federal criminal law reaches practically every kind of commercial or financial fraud. In addition, the federal criminal law reaches deeply into regulation of the environment, health care, and industrial work places. The Supreme Court is the ultimate appellate authority over federal criminal law.

The federal court system also has exclusive competence of proceedings for judicial review of federal administrative agencies. These agencies regulate the securities markets; telecommunications; banks; transportation by air, rail, and truck; food processing; drug research and manufacture; many aspects of labor relations; and environmental pollution. In addition, federal agencies administer a number of federal programs, such as Social Security, and the federal tax laws. The Supreme Court is the ultimate appellate authority in interpreting the legal standards by which federal administrative agencies are empowered to act.

The federal court system has primary, and in many instances exclusive, competence of civil actions to enforce private rights created by federal statute. Federal rights for civil redress have been created for victims of many legal wrongs, including the following: racial, gender, and age discrimination; commercial and financial fraud; patent and copyright infringement; antitrust violations; certain kinds of unfair business competition; unfair labor practices; and deprivations of due process by state and local governments. The federal courts also have competence in cases concerning use of federal lands, which constitute a substantial portion of the territory of the United States, and matters of admiralty and maritime jurisdiction. The Supreme Court is the ultimate appellate authority in all such litigation.

The Supreme Court has competence as an appellate court to review decisions of state courts that involve questions of federal law. Litigants in such cases must pursue appeal within the state courts before seeking appeal to the Supreme Court, but when state court appeal has been exhausted, a litigant may petition the Supreme Court to consider any federal question involved. This competence extends not only to civil actions in state courts but to state court criminal cases in which federal legal issues have arisen, such as violations of federal due process requirements.

In exercising its authority in this broad array of legal matters, the Supreme Court speaks as the final interpreter of the Constitution. As such it has appellate authority over federal administrative officials, authority to declare acts of Congress unconstitutional, and authority to direct the President of the United States to comply with the law—as in *United States v. Nixon,* which involved the question of whether the President must comply with a court order to produce documents. The Court has similar appellate authority concerning the validity under federal law of state legislation and acts of state and municipal officials.

These enormous legal powers are not explicitly stated in the Constitution. They were asserted in primal form in the seminal decision of *Marbury v. Madison* in 1803 and have been repeatedly reasserted and expanded in the nearly two centuries since. From time to time the Supreme Court's authority has been challenged. In 1832, for example, President Andrew Jackson reportedly said of one of the Court's very controversial decisions by Chief Justice Marshall: "John Marshall has made his decision: now let him enforce it!"[4] The American Civil War was in part a reaction against the Supreme Court's proslavery decision in *Dred Scott v. Sandford* in 1856.[5] Southern states defied the Supreme Court following its decision in *Brown v. Board of Education.* President Nixon left it doubtful for a time whether he would acquiesce in the Supreme Court's decision subjecting him to the order of a federal court. The product of these controversies, however, has been a strengthened public commitment to the legitimacy of the Supreme Court's authority and a corresponding acceptance of the authority in the lower federal and state courts.

The proceedings by which those courts function are primarily governed by the law of civil procedure. Hence the constitutional importance of the body of law discussed in this book.

CHAPTER FOUR

Concepts of Law and Legal Proof

As noted in chapter 1, a civil lawsuit depends upon resolution of questions of fact and questions of law. When a question of fact is in dispute, the issue is determined through the consideration of conflicting evidence. When a matter of law is in dispute, the issue is determined through the consideration of alternative interpretations of law. As we have also seen, in American civil cases a jury usually determines the issues of fact in cases involving claims for substantial damages. Moreover, the procedure for trying issues fact of in jury cases is the model for that in cases in which factual determinations are made by a judge. In contrast, in most other modern legal systems the issues of fact as well as the issues of law are decided by judges.

The division of function between judge and jury makes it necessary to maintain a corresponding distinction between issues of law and issues of fact. However, the distinction is to an important extent artificial. For example, in a case involving a contract for construction of a building, the key issue can be whether the work was completed according to acceptable standards. This issue can be considered one of law ("in a contract claim the promisee must prove performance on its part") or one of fact ("acceptable performance is the standard actually prevailing in the market"). Nevertheless, in American procedure this distinction defines the different roles of judge and jury. If the issue is classified as one of law, the resolution of that issue is for the judge; if it is classified as one of fact, its resolution is for the jury. However, the judge also decides issues of fact that arise in various preliminary matters such as discovery and disputes over jurisdiction.

In a jury case, the judge's task is to express the governing legal principles in instructing the jury about the law. The jury then applies these principles in weighing and drawing inferences from the evidence. In a nonjury case, the judge determines the governing legal principles and also decides the factual issues.

Viewed mechanically, factual issues are resolved by proof and legal issues are resolved by examining the law. The American system characteristically performs these functions using judge and jury in combination, while other legal systems perform them only through a judge. Formally, an American judge and a judge in a European legal system could trade places in a nonjury case and, with a little practice, perform with equal effect in either system.

However, the differences between legal systems go deeper. Ultimately, a system of justice reflects the political and social culture in which it is embedded. The nations of Europe each have their own distinctive characteristics: no one would mistake Italy for Germany, for example. So also French culture shapes the civil law system in France to a configuration different from the civil law system in either Germany or Italy. American political and social culture is well recognized as being different from that of Europe, Japan, or Latin America. The industrial democracies, although similar in their basic political economies, differ from each other in manifold subtle idiosyncracies—the product of national differences in history, language, ethnic composition, educational system, religious tradition, regional subdivision, constitutional structure, political organization, specific economic organization, and—not least—legal institutions.

Fully explicating such differences would require a depth of understanding to which cultural anthropology can only strive and to which legal analysis cannot pretend. Nevertheless, it is helpful to identify salient characteristics in the American legal culture that affect how American adjudication actually functions.

The State and the Government

Law is an exercise of authority as well as a quest for justice. The law of civil procedure is such an expression of authority, along with criminal procedure and the substantive civil and criminal law. In an immediate sense, the law's authority in civil procedure is personified by the judge and other litigation participants—the court attendants and clerks, the advocates, and, in the American system, the jury. The law's authority is also manifested in courtroom language and conventions of behavior. Courtroom language is technical and formal, expressed through highly structured conversations in which the speakers have fixed parts. (Sometimes a juror in an American trial, being inexperienced in the role, speaks out of turn, thereby causing amusement, consternation, and sometimes disruption.) The law's authority is also manifested in the fact that its judgments are enforceable by legalized coercion. A court's judgment thus is more than a pronouncement of justice according to law; if the losing party does not voluntarily comply with the judgment, government officials can impose compliance.

Behind these immediate manifestations of the law's authority is a more comprehensive, if somewhat amorphous, authority. It is accurate to say that the law expresses the authority of "society" or "the community" as a whole. However, in pragmatic terms this reference is question-begging. By what institutional mechanism does "the community" express itself as legal authority? In the premodern tradition, the law was considered to be the king's voice and legal procedure to be the king's justice. The same concept is reflected in the philosophy of legal positivism, expounded by such legal theorists as Hans Kelsen in the continental tradition and John Austin in the English tradition, which asserts that law is a command or commandment. But what is the nature of the authority from which the commandments emanate?

Legal philosophy has formulated at least two general answers to this question.[1] One answer conceives the law as a commandment issuing from the state: this conception predominates in the continental European tradition. The other conceives the law as expressing common understanding on the part of the body politic. This conception predominates in the common law tradition, particularly in its American version.

In the conception of law as a command from the state, the law's legitimacy fundamentally depends on the legitimacy of the state's governing apparatus, including the judicial system.

The "state" is a collective civic enterprise having a legal identity of its own—approximately an impersonation of a king—and exists independent of the presently incumbent officials who function on the state's behalf. The state also has an autonomous social purpose that should guide official action in administering the law as well as other governmental functions. In classical terminology, the state is a corporate being with identity distinct from and transcending that of its citizenry.

This conception of the state has practical implications in the administration of justice, particularly the responsibility of judges. In this conception, judges are considered to be—and consider themselves to be—primarily responsible to the state. This responsibility requires the judge to comprehend the state's intendment as expressed in the law. Deference to the state in principle precludes interjection of a judge's personal convictions of what the law should mean. By the same token, the judge's voice is that of the public corporate entity.[2] The judge's burden of individual responsibility is mitigated by this instrumental relationship and by the fact that decisions in serious cases require a judicial panel of three members. Without such mitigation, the burden of committing grave injustice, which is a constant occupational risk for judges, might be unbearable.

The American concept of law and of the judge is quite different. There is no concept of the "state"; the term *state* in American law refers to the fifty subordinate units in the federal system. Legal authority is instead a conjunction of the government, the people, and the law. The government is a set of officials who have specific and limited legal authority derived from laws enacted upon authority of the people, according to procedures specified in constitutions (the U.S. Constitution and state counterparts) that themselves confer specific and limited legal authority. The law consists of mutually binding rules pronounced collectively by the people, through representatives who give voice to the people's will. In classical terminology, the relationship is a *societas,* an association existing through the undertakings of its members and lacking any separate identity such as is connoted by the term *state.*

In principle, according to this conception, the law exists independent of any other authority and is intelligible to every citizen, because citizens are the ultimate authors of the law. Correlatively, while judges have office and functions authorized by law, they have no special access to the law or to the sources of the law's deeper meaning. A judge whose performance is derelict can be removed from office, like any other government official. By the same token, the law can be comprehended by the parties and by members of a jury, so long as the judge gives them helpful instruction about the law's technical aspects. The parties accordingly have authority to assert what the law's true meaning is, if necessary with the assistance of advocates.

The American conception of law and its administration has not only theoretical significance but also practical consequences. In American procedure the judge's function is participatory rather than central to the administration of the law, and salient parts are played by the jury and by the parties. In principle, the judge's responsibility is to respond to the parties' arguments about the true meaning of the law and to submit factual disputes to the jury. In cases where the judge decides the facts as well as the legal issues, the judge is a surrogate for the jury; the judge ascertains the applicable legal principles much as in instructing a jury, and then "finds" the facts in light of those principles. The judge has no fealty to a higher public authority, for no such authority exists independent of the law's expressions.

It should not be imagined that these different conceptions of law and the state are perfectly understood in these terms either in the United States or in legal systems of the European tradition. Nor is there agreement about these conceptualizations among legal scholars. However, in broad outline each conception reflects the ethos of a legal system—the preconceptions of its structure and character—and these animate the way justice is administered.

Legal Reasoning

Legal rules are applied through a mental process that addresses the relationship between legal concepts and the circumstances of a specific case, whereby a conclusion may be reached in favor of one party or the other. This process is called legal reasoning.

Legal reasoning is above all practical. It is conducted in contemplation of an award of judgment, not merely the resolution of a hypothetical case or provision of admonitory advice. There is a real-world winner and a loser. An award of judgment is the basis for an involuntary allocation of wealth between the parties, either denying plaintiff an entitlement or ordering that defendant fulfill such an entitlement. Moreover, legal reasoning usually is employed in cases where the justice of the matter is doubtful. Disputes in which the parties' legal rights are clear do not ordinarily come to trial, being settled at some preliminary stage, or are not initiated in the first place. Thus, legal reasoning is a process for definitively deciding a dispute that is to some extent legally or factually indeterminate.

Legal reasoning consists of both an internal mental process and communication to others.[3] In their internal mental processes, the members of the tribunal form impressions of the evidence and normative ideas for assessing its significance. However, one can never fully explicate one's own thoughts, and in this respect legal reasoning is as opaque as practical reasoning directed to any other purpose. It incorporates perception, interpretation of circumstances, vocational background and training, lifetime personal experience, normative ideals including but not limited to legal rules, awareness of the attitudes of others, foresight as to consequences, interpretive trial and error, and no little confusion. In arriving at a decision the members of the tribunal—whether judges or jurors—talk to each other about the case as best they can, and thereby come to a collective decision.

Communication to others, particularly the parties and the public, comes after a decision is reached. In the civil law system, the court's decision must be a written discussion of the facts and the applicable law. A similar kind of communication occurs in the American system when a judge decides a case without a jury. In a case tried to a jury, however, the communication is provided in two disconnected parts: the judge's instructions to the jury, which form the legal premises that are supposed to govern the jury, and the jury's verdict, which is simply a statement of outcome for one side or the other. The jury necessarily engages in some kind of thought process in reaching a verdict, but ordinarily a jury is neither required nor permitted to explain its thought process.

Even when a judge explains the basis of decision in a case tried without a jury, however, the explanation is necessarily incomplete. The actual mental process of a judge or jury cannot be ascertained from an external perspective and the court's internal mental process is necessarily somewhat different from the formal terms in which the court's decision is expressed. The legal system presumes that there is a direct and logical relationship between the court's thought process and its conclusion, and recognizes that having to make a decision is a mental discipline of its own. As a practical matter a legal system can demand no more.

The process of legal reasoning nevertheless depends in part on the decision maker's preconception of law itself. In the civil law system, for example, the law is conceived as a comprehensive and definitive text. It consists of a code systematically organized by subject matter and considered to speak in one consistent voice at every moment in time. In principle, the disputes to which the law applies have always been embraced by the law's eternal omniscience.

The rhetoric of judicial justification in the civil law system follows from this conception. The model of justification is deductive, whereby the law is considered to have anticipated the circumstances revealed in the case and the court's task is to discern the result that the law has foreordained. Since the law expresses itself in legal categories, the court's basic task is to identity the appropriate general category and then to state how the specific case is subsumed in that category. Thus, the justification for judgment in a motor vehicle accident case might proceed as follows: the law governing the operation of motor vehicles states that a driver must proceed at a reasonable speed under the circumstances; the present circumstances involve driving at unreasonable speed in that traffic was heavy and the conditions dark and rainy; therefore, the driver was guilty of driving at unreasonable speed.

In the common law system, particularly its American version, the law is considered to be a continually evolving historical phenomenon. While the law can be stated as a comprehensive text at any given time, it is understandable primarily in terms of its historical development rather than its conceptual content. Since history is a synthesis of concrete experience, law is a similar synthesis. In the phrase of Justice Oliver Wendell Holmes, "The life of the law has not been logic, it has been experience." In the American conception, therefore, law is dynamic, incomplete, and reformative in spirit and direction. Moreover, the American conception reflects a strong individualistic and moralistic predisposition. Law is cast in terms of legal rights rather than legal obligations; it is a set of protections for autonomy of the individual, rather than a set of obligations that the citizen owes to society.

In American terms, the justification for a judgment involving motor vehicle case involving an accusation of unreasonable speed could proceed as follows: The statute adopts the community's standard of reasonable conduct. Whether the driver was proceeding at a reasonable speed depends on all the circumstances—the location of the road, the conditions of traffic, the weather, the time of day, and the errand upon which the driver was about. The evidence indicates that the traffic was heavy and the conditions dark and rainy. In these circumstances, others had a right to expect that the driver would drive more slowly and carefully. Therefore, the plaintiff should be entitled to recover compensation.

Concepts of Proof

When factual issues arise in litigation, they are resolved by consideration of evidence. Evidence consists of testimony of witnesses, documents such as contracts and deeds, and occasionally physical objects. In assessing the evidence in a given case, the key problem may be determining what events actually occurred. For example, two observers of an event may give inconsistent accounts, so that the credibility of their testimony must be assessed. Alternatively, the key problem may be determining the significance of uncontested evidence. For example, in litigation over a construction contract it may be agreed that the building was constructed in a particular way but disputed whether that conformed to the specifications called for in the contract.

Generally speaking, the process for determining factual issues in litigation is the same as that used by people in their ordinary affairs. When the accounts of witnesses differ, the truth is judged by estimating the witnesses' opportunities to observe, the apparent trustworthiness of their recall, and their possible bias in one direction or another. Also significant is the inherent plausibility of their accounts, judged by experience in everyday life. Making factual determinations in litigation differs only in that a court's decision about facts may not be appealed by some nonjudicial recourse.

In certain kinds of factual issues, the tribunal may have the assistance of expert witnesses. The function of an expert witness is to interpret evidence whose significance is not fully apparent to a person without specialized knowledge. For example, in a case involving personal injuries, medical expert testimony may help the court determine the extent of the victim's injuries and the probabilities for eventual restoration to health. So also, in international transactions experts may be required to translate documents or to witness testimony received in a foreign language. The use of experts by the courts is essentially similar to the use of expertise in other contexts. For example, a family doctor whose practice consists of general diagnosis may consult a specialist when the patient's symptoms are difficult to interpret; the specialist's evaluation can help in arriving at a better-informed determination of the issue in question.

The evidence may be more or less equally balanced, in which event a rule is needed to direct a decision. Every legal system has auxiliary rules to guide the court in such circumstances—the rules governing burden of proof. The effect of a burden of proof rule is that the party having the burden as to a particular issue of fact will lose on that issue if the court determines that the evidence is evenly balanced. Putting the point somewhat differently, if the court cannot determine the fact from the evidence, then the issue is resolved against the party with the burden of proof. The plaintiff usually has the burden of proof concerning the principal elements of a legal grievance.

Whatever the burden of proof rules, there is also an element of initial predisposition or sympathy or prejudice in the outlook of every decision maker. It is here that the significance of jury trial reveals itself. In most cases, juries and judges agree in their assessments of evidence: where a judge would find for defendant against plaintiff, a jury usually will do so as well, and vice versa. However, when the evidence is in conflict, differences between judge and jury tend to arise where the plaintiff is an ordinary person with a morally sympathetic case and the opposing party is part of the "establishment," such as a large business corporation, a government agency, or an individual who is a high-status professional. On the other hand, judges tend to be somewhat more favorable to plaintiffs in certain kinds of cases involving large economic losses. As will be explained in chapter 7, the jury is not permitted to decide upon the evidence unless the judge considers the evidence sufficient to permit a rational finding. However, if the evidence meets this standard, a jury may decide for one party although the judge would decide for the other.

The differences in how juries and judges decide closely balanced cases ultimately reflect the fact that jurors have somewhat different life experience from judges. For example, ordinary citizens generally are not treated as respectfully by persons in authority as judges are treated. This experience affects how ordinary citizens, sitting as jurors, interpret testimony by persons in authority. Judges deal with legal controversies day in and day out, and may become inured to routine legal hardship; most jurors experience the law in a very different way. Judges have had legal training, whereas jurors have a layman's sense of justice. (Today lawyers are permitted to serve on juries, and sometimes do so.) In close cases, such differences in outlook can be determinative.

That the same evidence can lead jurors and judges to different conclusions is intrinsic to American civil procedure. Indeed, preserving jury trial would have no purpose if there were no such difference. Much of American civil procedure is built around this phenomenon, as we shall explain further in later chapters.

A more theoretical difference between the American conception of evidence and that in the civil law system stems from the fact that the civil law system regards the judge as an expert in evaluating evidence, while the American system regards the judge as substituting for a lay jury in evaluating evidence. The intellectual tradition of civil law scholarship treats the task of factual analysis as involving a technical rigor no less exacting than legal analysis. The method of legal training in the civil law centers on deductive analysis, which is assumed to be equally applicable to legal reasoning and to factual analysis. In contrast, the American system rests on the premise that assessment of evidence involves no special expertise. By definition, in a jury case the evidence is assessed by minds untrained in law; it would be a contradiction to say that legal training is required to analyze facts when jurors do so without any such training. Moreover, judges in the American system have no special judicial training before appointment to the bench, nor are they systematically trained within the court system or promoted on the basis of experience. When it comes to factual determinations, therefore, the judge in the American system is regarded as having no special insight.

Truth and Justice

The most difficult problem that the administration of justice confronts is the inevitable risk of committing injustice by relying on evidence that is in fact untrue. Various mechanisms can be devised to reduce this risk. One is to require especially reliable evidence to sustain a claim. For example, written documentation may be required in order to prove certain types of transactions, such as transferring of ownership of real estate. Another mechanism is to impose an extra burden of proof concerning certain issues, such as "clear and convincing evidence" rather than merely "a preponderance of the evidence."

Another device for dealing with uncertain evidence is simply to deny a legal remedy for certain types of wrongs, even though they are morally obnoxious, because the usual sources of proof of that type of wrong are regarded as unreliable. For example, many states disallow claims against decedent's estates unless they are corroborated in writing or by testimony of independent witnesses.

All developed legal systems use these devices in various combinations. However, their effect is inevitably to deny justice in certain cases. For example, if written documentation is required in order that an agreement to sell land be legally enforceable, where an agreement to sell land has actually been made through an oral promise, there will be a denial of justice when that agreement is not enforced. On the other hand, if written documentation is not rigorously required, the legal system will inevitably be subjected to claims based on oral testimony that is in fact false. So also, the special heavy burden of proof in criminal cases—"beyond a reasonable doubt"—means that many who are in fact guilty will nevertheless be let go free. Such is the sad experience of the law through the ages.

The legal system has no way of avoiding this dilemma, for no legal procedure can always discern the truth. Hence, any device designed to affect the weight of evidence reflects a balance between the aim of doing justice according to the actual facts of specific transactions and the aim of protecting the system of justice from abusive claims and defenses. Some misassessments of facts will occur whatever the rule, resulting in corresponding injustice. The problem is how to balance the risks.

Legal systems address these risks with different balances that reflect underlying social values, specific legal tradition, and to some extent self-fulfilling prophecy. For example, if a legal system requires written documentation in certain transactions, it may be inferred that parties who have not committed an agreement to writing intended that the transaction not be binding until it was put in writing. In general, the American legal system has faith that triers of fact can find the truth. Accordingly, it imposes requirements for special proof in only a few types of cases.

This liberality toward disputable evidence has important effects on the kinds of civil cases brought. The rule having greatest practical effect is that which allows an interested party to be a witness in his or her own behalf. For example, in an automobile accident in which two drivers are injured, each driver may make a claim for injuries based on the other driver's fault. Under American law, both drivers are competent as witnesses. So also, a person claiming injury as a result of having eaten contaminated food is competent to testify about what happened to him or her. In contrast, in many civil law countries the law of evidence precludes plaintiffs and defendants from testifying, on the premise that their interest in the outcome will bias their testimony. Although this preclusion of party testimony may surprise the modern American mind, it was the rule at common law until the nineteenth century.

The effect of the modern American rule concerning party testimony is enormous, for it makes possible the prosecution of many kinds of claims that would otherwise fail for lack of evidence. Illustrative are two-car motor vehicle cases, where the participants usually are the only available witnesses to indicate who was at fault. The same is true of claims resulting from alleged defects in manufactured products such as canned or frozen food, drugs, and machinery, and of all kinds of claims based on agreements that were not reduced to writing. In contrast, in most other countries claims of this kind cannot be prosecuted because of the limitations on permissible evidence. This also means that compensation for auto accidents cannot be afforded through civil damages litigation but requires other legal solutions, such as medical and disability insurance. It would be a mistake to conclude that these larger social solutions derive directly from rules of evidence; however, it would also be a mistake to ignore the significance of the evidence rules.

American procedural law has a similar liberality toward proof of business transactions through oral testimony. Perhaps the most astonishing example is the ten-billion-dollar judgment in the 1980s in favor of Pennzoil Company against Texaco, for interference with an agreement by which Pennzoil was to buy Getty Oil Company. Texaco contended that there was no agreement between Pennzoil and Getty because the negotiations had not been committed to a final written contract. However, proof of an oral agreement was legally sufficient. Less dramatic cases involving oral agreements are routine; much American commercial litigation involves oral testimony that contradicts written documentation. Most business people from other countries, and many Americans as well, regard this practice as ridiculous and dangerous to orderly commerce.

Another major difference between American law and civil law systems concerns the significance of intent, a difference in substantive law that has major procedural significance. "Intent" refers to the mental state accompanying conduct: intentional infliction of injury is more serious that unintentional, and reckless disregard of consequences is more serious than simple inattention. American law attaches great significance to intent in all kinds of transactions— commercial, financial, consumer, and dispositions of family property; the civil law tends to define legal consequences of conduct in terms of effects rather than of intent. For this reason, it is much more often relevant in American law to determine intent and therefore much more often necessary to search out evidence of intent. Largely for this reason, American litigation involving business transactions finds the parties delving into boxes and boxes of business correspondence and files, searching for evidence about what various corporate employees knew or should have known. In civil law litigation most evidence of this kind would be irrelevant, the court being concerned only with the formal nature of the parties' relationship, whether contractual or otherwise. Indeed, in civil law procedure, efforts to obtain private business files for use in a civil case would be regarded as an invasion of privacy. To oversimplify, American law considers circumstantial evidence of the parties' knowledge and intent to be of the essence, while the civil law regards such evidence as unreliable and usually of secondary significance.

American law's receptivity to party testimony and evidence of party intent reflects underlying social values. The attitude favors the relatively less educated against those who are better educated, because better educated people are more aware of legal rules concerning proof and generally can more readily arrange their transactions accordingly. It favors consumers against sellers for similar reasons. Perhaps above all, it reflects faith in the ability of juries to find the truth in the face of conflicting evidence, and to tell good guys from bad guys.

CHAPTER FIVE

Lawyers and the Adversary System

Civil litigation in the United States is presented and defended primarily by advocates for the parties, with the judge serving in a relatively passive role. Theoretically, the parties bear the entire responsibility for presenting the law and the facts; the judge is obliged merely to affirm or reject the parties' contentions. For this reason the American system is called the adversary system. Most other modern legal systems employ what is usually called the inquisitorial system, meaning only that the initiative rests with the judge for developing the facts of a case and the governing legal principles.

In practice, however, neither system fully corresponds to its theoretical model. In the civil law system the judge has dominant authority to determine the legal theory to be applied, but the judge is highly dependent on the parties for presentation of the evidence. The civil law judge has authority to investigate the facts on the judge's own initiative, but in most countries this authority is conservatively exercised. Common law judges have authority to initiate inquiry into the evidence but rarely exercise it. In this sense, both systems depend on adversary presentations so far as the facts are concerned, notwithstanding the theoretical differences between their conceptions of the judge's role.

Except in small claims cases, in modern litigation the function of presenting a party's case is performed by a lawyer.

In the early common law, the parties themselves presented their positions to the court. The controversies coming before the common law courts at that time involved landlords of substance and other people generally able to fend for themselves in litigation. Even so, litigants found it convenient to have advice from court attendants familiar with the ways of the court and available to assure against procedural mishap. Those who made such appearances for the parties were called attorneys, meaning party agents. Use of an attorney was convenient but was not legally obligatory. In modern American litigation, use of an attorney is still not legally obligatory. Litigants who cannot afford to retain an attorney, or who do not wish to do so, are entitled to present their cases personally—*in propria persona*. The procedure in small claims court, discussed in chapter 8, is designed to accommodate parties who participate personally. For the most part, however, employing an attorney in civil litigation is a practical necessity.

An attorney's expertise includes technical knowledge of the law, skill in developing and presenting evidence, and familiarity with the work habits of the courts. The value of such expertise is evident, for, as this book makes clear, American civil justice is complicated. Litigants who attempt to act for themselves often have as much difficulty with the mechanics of presenting a case as with the effective presentation of its merits.

The principle that advocates are agents for the parties has important corollaries. An advocate must be given specific authority by the client in order to commence a suit and to enter a defense, to approve a settlement, and to waive important procedural rights, such as the right to jury trial and the right to take an appeal. However, the attorney has broad authority in matters of strategy and tactics—for example, decisions as to which witnesses to call and what lines of questioning to pursue. Correlatively, a party ordinarily is bound by his attorney's strategic and tactical decisions. Generally speaking, the parties and not the attorneys are responsible for costs incurred in the litigation.

The Adversary System

In practice, the advocates assume primary responsibility for conducting the litigation. Conscientious advocates are careful to keep their clients fully advised, although it is a widespread complaint that lawyers are inattentive to these responsibilities. Whether or not they consult with their clients, however, the advocates are the architects of the litigation. The plaintiff's advocate decides upon the legal theories on which the complaint should be based, the discovery to be conducted, the evidence to be presented at trial, and the thematic concept of the case. The advocate for the defense has counterpart responsibilities.

These are heavy responsibilities. The selection of legal theories itself is often a complex task. Federal and state statutory, decisional, and constitutional law all can be applicable to a specific case; sometimes the plaintiff can choose between federal and state court as the forum for the litigation, itself an important strategic consideration. Developing the evidence often requires extensive investigation. Prospective witnesses have to be located, questioned, and invited to give their evidence; and in litigation arising from business transactions, the client's files must be sifted for relevant documents. Where expert testimony is required, competent and effective experts must be retained. If diagrams, maps, charts, or accounting summaries will be useful exhibits at trial, they are worked up under the advocate's direction.

The advocate conducts the pretrial discovery against the opposing party. As developed more fully in chapter 6, this involves taking the depositions of potential witnesses, including the opposing party, and identifying and inspecting relevant documents in the opposing party's possession. In complicated business litigation, thousands of such documents must be reviewed and analyzed. Discovery may require weeks or months of the advocate's effort, sometimes over the course of years before the anticipated trial date.

At trial, the advocates are responsible for presenting evidence for their respective clients, attacking the opposing party's evidence, and arguing the case to the court and jury. In principle, the judge is required only to observe and to rule on objections that each advocate may address to the presentations by the other.

The Judge as Umpire

The judge in American civil procedure generally has only secondary initiative in the conduct of the case. Some judges are almost wholly passive. At the pretrial stage they give attention to a case only when a motion by a party requires them to make a ruling, and then they simply rule one way or the other without explanation. Other judges are very active, exploring the case early in the litigation, inviting motions that will clarify or resolve critical issues, intervening if discovery has become contentious or delayed, and organizing the presentations at trial. The judge may exercise "sound judicial discretion" concerning the nature and extent of his or her participation, so long as the judge discharges minimum judicial responsibilities and does not "assume the role of an advocate." A judgment will be reversed for the judge's mishandling a trial only in extreme situations, either where total confusion descended or where the advocates were denied their opportunity to be heard.

Nevertheless, even relatively activist judges are limited in their scope of initiative, compared with that vested in judges of the civil law system. A judge in the American system ordinarily does not develop the legal theories of the case, but only responds to contentions presented by the parties. The judge does not identify potentially relevant evidence, but only monitors the presentations of evidence by the parties. The judge does not conduct the primary examination of witnesses, nor their cross-examination; at most, the judge asks supplemental questions when the advocates have concluded their questioning. The judge ordinarily does not pursue possibilities for gathering additional evidence. If the proof is legally insufficient, the judge rules against the party with the burden of proof.

At the close of the trial, the judge ordinarily does not review the evidence in detail for the jury but defers in that function to the advocates. In a case without a jury, the judge accepts argument by the advocates but is not required to recapitulate the evidence in reaching a decision. When facts are found by a jury, ordinarily their finding takes the form of a conclusory verdict, for example: "We find for the plaintiff in the amount of (for example] fifty thousand dollars," or, "We find for the defendant." Thereupon, the court's judgment is entered in the same terms, without further explanation or stated justification. When facts are found by the judge, the decision may include an extensive explanation of the judge's conclusions, but this is not required. The rules require no more than a skeletal statement of the ultimate conclusions, and a trial court's decisions usually go no further than this requirement.

Lawyers and Professional Ethics

Because the role of the attorney is central to the adversary system, something should be said about the American legal profession.

As is well known, the lawyer population in the United States is very large. There are over 750,000 licensed lawyers, one for about every three hundred people in the general population. About half of these practice either alone or in firms of two or three lawyers. However, most substantial litigation and virtually all major litigation is conducted by law firms.

Upon admission to practice, a lawyer is licensed to serve as both advocate and legal counselor. There is no division of the profession between barristers and solicitors, as in England. The requirements for admission to practice law include completion of general education at the university level; completion of a three-year postgraduate law school curriculum; passing a two- or three-day written bar examination; and proof of satisfactory character, the latter requirement being minimal. Many law graduates seek as their first employment a position with a public agency, for example, the prosecutor's office. Others seek positions as assistants with established practitioners or with business corporations. Students with good academic records, and those from prestigious law schools, find positions with law firms as employees. Law firms are usually organized as partnerships, whose members are compensated by shares in the firm's net revenues. Beginning lawyers are usually paid a salary.

The range of competence among American lawyers is very great. The minimum academic requirements for entry into law school are modest and there is great variation in the intensity of legal training among law schools and in the practical training for newly admitted lawyers within law firms. The best American advocates are extraordinary in resourcefulness, energy, and thoroughness. Many lawyers who appear in court, however, are poorly prepared, confused in their purpose, and inept in forensic technique.

Law firms are usually specialized in the types of litigation that they undertake. Some firms do not handle criminal cases, for example, except those incidental to representation of business enterprises. In certain fields of civil litigation, notably personal injury cases, lawyers specialize in representing either claimants or defendants. There is a parallel structure in business litigation, although such litigation for both plaintiffs and defendants may be handled by firms of various size. Some law firms have hundreds of lawyers in offices located in major cities across the country.

The legal profession is regulated primarily by state law, although the federal courts exercise authority over lawyers appearing in litigation before them. The governing regulations include codes of professional ethics; duties and responsibilities imposed by the law of procedure; and common law rules. This body of law is usually called the law of professional responsibility.

Each state has a code of professional ethics that defines the lawyer's responsibilities in representing clients. These provisions vary somewhat from state to state but in essentials are quite the same throughout the country. Most states, and the federal courts as well, have adopted the Rules of Professional Conduct, a code of ethical rules that has been formulated by the American Bar Association. The ABA is the national voluntary association of the legal profession in the United States. It has no direct legal authority in governance of the profession, but it exercises substantial leadership influence. Principal authority in matters of professional discipline is vested in the courts of the respective states. There are bar associations in each state, which assist the courts in regulating the profession.

The Rules of Professional Conduct cover most aspects of a lawyer's professional responsibilities, including the duties of loyalty to clients and avoidance of conflicts of interest; the duty to maintain the secrecy of confidential information obtained from clients; duties toward opposing parties in litigation and negotiations; responsibilities of supervising lawyers and partners in law firms concerning ethical practice by subordinate lawyers; and duties of advocates to the courts.

In the adversary system, the lawyer's duties to the court are delicately balanced with responsibilities to the client. On behalf of the client, the advocate must act zealously and faithfully. This requires the advocate to present all favorable evidence, to mitigate unfavorable evidence by cross-examination and argument, and to advance the most favorable interpretation of the law. A lawyer should not disclose adverse evidence except as required by the rules of procedure, including the rules governing pretrial discovery. In deference to the court, however, the advocate must not present evidence that he knows to be false, for example, testimony of a witness he knows to be lying. The advocate has authority to refuse to offer evidence that he believes is false, even if the client wishes such evidence to be introduced. The advocate must advise the court of authoritative legal sources of which the court is unaware. Finally, the lawyer is obliged to be truthful in all statements made to the court of his own knowledge. For example, a lawyer may not seek a delay of proceedings based on a false statement that he has been called away by an emergency.

In practice, these ethical responsibilities are often imperfectly fulfilled. The adversary system subjects the advocates to great incentives to ignore the duty to the court in favor of the interest of the client. Perhaps the most sensitive problem arises in the preparation of testimony, including the client's own testimony. The advocate is permitted to consult confidentially with the client and other favorable witnesses concerning their anticipated testimony in discovery and at trial. In such conversations, the lawyer is not permitted to advise the witness of the testimony to be given, for that would constitute fabrication of evidence. However, the lawyer is permitted to probe the witness's memory and, if the witness is verbally inarticulate, to suggest how the witness might express his account of the events. The distinction between these approaches to a witness is at best subtle and at worst the basis for pretense. A conscientious lawyer can interview a witness without significantly distorting the witness's recollection, and indeed can often properly clarify it. On the other hand, a manipulative lawyer, while pretending an interview, can contrive testimony for a suggestible or unscrupulous witness.

Direct contact by the advocate with witnesses other than the client is not permitted in most countries. Many critics consider that the American practice of permitting an advocate to interview witnesses invites perversion of testimonial evidence. Furthermore, the rule allowing direct interview of witnesses assumes that the narrative of a witness's recollection is unaffected by the circumstances under which the recollection is given. That assumption is of course contradicted by the premises of the adversary system itself, which hold that truth can be produced only through bilateral party interrogation of witnesses. The permission to interview witnesses directly reflects an extreme commitment to the principle of party presentation and also extreme optimism about the integrity of lawyers and witnesses. The adversary system would still be preserved if the rules required that pretrial interviews be conducted in the presence of a monitor. Reform to this effect has been proposed from time to time, to no avail.

The conduct of the advocates in the adversary system is also governed by the rules of civil procedure. Generally speaking, these rules confer powers on the advocates, while the rules of ethics impose controls on the exercise of those powers. Thus, the advocate's right to select the legal theory for his case, and to present the evidence in its support, is subject to the ethical controls on how these procedural powers are to be exercised. The rules of procedure, however, also contain many controls.

Among these controls is the procedural rule that any communication by an advocate to the court must be disclosed to all opposing parties. For example, when a written pretrial motion is filed with the court, the procedural rules require that a full copy must be provided to opposing parties. The same principle applies to oral presentations to the court. A corresponding ethical rule prohibits communications between an advocate for one party and the court except in the presence of the advocates for all parties. Another procedural control is the pretrial discovery procedure. Although an advocate may conduct unilateral discussions with prospective witnesses, opposing parties may depose those witnesses before trial. A deposition consists of questioning under oath that is recorded verbatim, which may be pursued aggressively and in detail. The witness's responses may later be used in cross-examination at trial. The effect of a deposition is usually to commit the witness to the recollection given in the deposition testimony and to mitigate the effects of prior informal discussions between the witness and the opposing advocate. Other procedural controls on advocates will be considered in chapter 6, concerning pretrial procedure, and in chapter 7, concerning the trial.

There is also a body of common law governing the lawyer's responsibilities. Common law rules regulate the contractual relationship between the advocate and the client—for example, whether the retainer fee covers only negotiation or also requires the lawyer to undertake litigation. Delegation of authority by the client to the lawyer is also governed by contract principles, subject to certain limitations imposed by the rules of ethics. Common law principles confer broad inherent authority on the court to supervise the conduct of litigation, enforceable by the power of contempt of court. This power is discussed in chapter 10.

The Civil Litigation Team

Modern litigation is usually conducted by teams, typically consisting of at least two lawyers, one or more paralegals, secretarial assistants, and consultants.

The head of the team is the lawyer who will present the case at trial; a junior lawyer usually is given primary responsibility for pretrial preparation. The pretrial tasks include doing legal research, investigating facts, conducting discovery, retaining and consulting with experts, preparing and arguing pretrial motions, and preparing witnesses and documents for presentation at trial. In very large cases, several lawyers will assist in both the trial and pretrial stages, and it is not uncommon for each side to have a team of five or six lawyers. In a complex case with multiple parties, the courtroom may be filled with the lawyers.

Paralegal assistants are people who are not lawyers but who have been trained in specialized litigation tasks. Some firms specializing in personal injury litigation, for example, have people trained as nurses to interview the injured parties about the extent of injuries and to analyze medical and hospital records. Firms engaged in business litigation have assistants trained in reading through files and classifying documents. With computer information systems, the contents of all documents can be sorted according to various parameters.

Many paralegal services are obtained from independent contractors rather than from law firm employees. For example, witness interviews may be conducted by special private investigators. Trial presentation often involves graphics, such as site diagrams in accident cases or transaction flow charts in commercial litigation. These may be prepared under the lawyer's direction by independent paralegal specialists.

Another kind of paralegal service is that provided by experts in various fields. In addition to giving testimony, confidential experts may be retained to analyze the case and to determine what kind of expert trial witness to retain. Law firms specializing in financial and commercial litigation often will have available a consultant accountant to help analyze complicated transactions.

The use of teamwork greatly expands the advocate's scope and technical facility in preparing and presenting litigation. It also greatly increases the cost, resulting in expenses that can be justified only when large stakes are involved. A big case is often likened to a theatrical production, and with good reason.

Fees, Costs, and Cost Sanctions

American civil litigation is strongly influenced by two unique rules concerning attorneys' fees and costs. The first is the "American rule" concerning allocation of the costs of litigation between the winner and loser. According to this rule, each party bears its own expenses, including attorneys' fees, unless special rules provide otherwise. This contrasts with the rule in most other legal systems, under which the losing party must pay the winner's litigation expenses, or a substantial portion of them. The second unique American rule is that contingent fees are permitted. Under a contingent-fee agreement, the lawyer receives no compensation for services in the case except an agreed-upon share if there is a recovery. Contingent fees are the normal arrangement in plaintiffs' personal injury cases and in certain types of financial and commercial litigation. They are rarely used on the defense side of civil cases.

The rules governing allocation of fees between winner and loser have incentive effects on the prosecution and defense of civil litigation. These effects are greatest on claims that are legally uncertain. Where a claim is very tenuous, there usually is little incentive to prosecute it; where a claim is very strong, there is usually little incentive to defend it. Where the legal strength of the claim is uncertain, however, the parties must calculate the cost of winning or losing in deciding whether and on what terms to settle their dispute.

The plaintiff's calculation will take account of both the prospect of losing and the prospect of winning. Theoretical analysis suggests that a plaintiff who cannot afford the additional loss of paying the opposing party's attorney's fees will be more hesitant to bring suit. Correlatively, under the American rule, where this risk is absent, a plaintiff who cannot afford additional loss is less inhibited from bringing suit. This in turn suggests that the American rule, all other things being equal, tends to favor claimants of limited means as compared with the rule prevailing in other systems.

Under a contingent-fee arrangement, the lawyer invests the necessary time in preparing and presenting the case. By customary practice, the lawyer in a contingent-fee arrangement also pays for auxiliary litigation expenses, such as discovery costs and expert witness fees. The standard contingency agreement is that the lawyer receives one-third of the recovery, whether by judgment or settlement, plus reimbursement of the litigation expenses the lawyer has underwritten. In effect, the contingent-fee agreement makes the claimant's lawyer a coventurer with the client in the prosecution of the claim. It is for this reason that contingent fees are prohibited in most legal systems, since their effect is that the lawyer purchases an interest in litigation. However, the contingency arrangement enables impecunious claimants to obtain the services of very able attorneys, whose fees they could not otherwise pay.

There are important exceptions to the foregoing rules and practices. Many statutes for protection of individual rights provide that a winning plaintiff many recover attorneys' fees in addition to damages. Such are the provisions, for example, of federal statutes prohibiting employment discrimination on account of race, religion, sex, or age, and of state consumer protection statutes. The antitrust laws provide for attorneys' fees for a winning plaintiff, as do some other "public interest" litigation statutes. Interestingly, very few of these statutes allow a successful defendant to recover attorneys' fees.

Parties to a contract may stipulate provisions for allocating attorneys' fees if litigation eventuates. Thus, a contract may provide that, in the event of litigation arising from the contract, the prevailing party shall recover attorneys' fees as well as such damages as may be awarded. Provisions to this effect are commonly included in agreements prepared by parties in strong bargaining positions, such as lenders and landlords. These provisions to some extent offset the American rule that would otherwise apply.

Still another exception occurs in cases where indigent litigants are provided legal aid. There is a constitutional requirement that counsel be provided to an indigent accused in a criminal case, and a similar requirement in juvenile court proceedings. However, in most states there is no such requirement in civil cases. Accordingly, legal aid is available only to persons who demonstrate financial need, under very stringent standards. Eligibility is usually determined by the legal aid service; only in rare instances in civil cases does a court determine that a litigant should be provided with public legal aid. There are no national standards for legal aid eligibility, and in many communities legal assistance may be obtained only by the very poor. The types of cases in which legal aid is provided are also limited. They usually include tenant evictions, debtor distress, and marriage dissolution. Legal aid attorneys generally are competent in their field, but have excessive caseloads and are poorly compensated.

In addition to attorneys' fees, litigation entails other expenses, including the support services already mentioned—law office staff, paralegals, experts, and so forth. Discovery depositions require an official reporter to record the testimony and to prepare the written transcription. This is a highly skilled art, requiring corresponding compensation for the court reporters. Litigation involving parties from different localities may require expensive travel. There are court fees as well, but these are generally nominal, out of concern that justice not be expensive. Such sensitivity to the public's expense for assisting civil litigation is anomalous, given the very large expenses that the parties usually have to bear.

In 1983, an important modification was made in the federal courts concerning attorneys' fees. The change was made in Rule 11 of the Federal Rules of Civil Procedure; several states have adopted similar modifications. Rule 11 requires that an attorney make reasonable pretrial investigation of facts in a case and assert legal positions only if they can be supported by reasonable legal argument. Such a requirement has long been imposed, but without effective sanctions. The 1983 amendment to Rule 11 provides that violation of this requirement is a basis for imposing on the violator the attorneys' fees incurred by the opposing party in contesting the unreasonable claim. The rule has been controversial and its effects debatable. It has been contended that enforcement of the rule has been harsh against civil rights plaintiffs, but the evidence for this claim is indeterminate. In any event, the rule has restrained some frivolous litigation. However, its overall effect on the volume and intensity of civil litigation has been insignificant.

Civil Litigation as a Law Enforcement Mechanism

Civil litigation is an important mechanism of law enforcement in the United States, particularly in the regulation of business activities. Businesses are governed by a broad array of regulatory provisions, such as financial disclosure, health and safety of employees, environmental controls, and consumer protection regulations. These regulatory provisions are enforced by various mechanisms, including reports to government, inspection of business records by government officials, administrative enforcement procedures, and criminal prosecution. Many regulatory provisions are also enforced by civil proceedings for recovery of monetary or injunctive relief. Some proceedings of this type are brought by a government agency as plaintiff, seeking recovery of money as a "civil penalty" or an injunction ordering the defendant to refrain from continued violation of the applicable regulations. Many regulatory statutes also authorize private victims to bring civil enforcement actions. The plaintiff in such actions is colloquially called a "private attorney general," meaning that a private party is acting like an attorney for the government.

Regulatory civil actions offer significant advantages compared with criminal prosecution and administrative agency enforcement.

Although criminal prosecution can result in imprisonment while a civil regulatory action cannot, criminal proceedings are governed by much more exacting procedural requirements. Criminal prosecution typically requires proof that violation was knowing, which is often difficult to obtain, and the proof standard is "beyond a reasonable doubt," which also is difficult to establish. Indigent defendants have the right to be provided counsel in criminal cases but not in civil ones. Juries, and many judges as well, are often reluctant to convict in a criminal case for an offense whose consequences are not obvious and immediate. Administrative agency enforcement is generally similar to that in a civil action. However, enforcement agencies often have inadequate staff for comprehensive prosecution, and may be under political pressure to be lenient toward offenders, or to avoid embarrassing the government itself.

For all these reasons, civil litigation is an important law enforcement mechanism. A civil enforcement action by a government agency is brought in the ordinary courts like an ordinary private lawsuit. For example, where a government agency determines that a business has persistently violated regulations governing employee rights or consumer protection, it may bring an action seeking an injunction and monetary penalties against the offending business. In some instances, it may also seek reparations for the victims of the violations.

Civil actions by private-party victims of regulatory violations usually seek damages, because this remedy creates a fund from which the plaintiff's advocate can be compensated, usually on a contingent-fee basis. A private-party enforcement action is conducted in all respects like an ordinary civil action, except that the statutory schemes generally provide that a successful plaintiff will be awarded attorneys' fees as well as other remedies.

Whether regulatory enforcement through private civil action is socially desirable is sometimes debated. However, the mechanism is a firmly established American legal institution and the political tendency in recent years has been to enlarge its use. This tendency reflects skepticism about the effectiveness of government agencies, hope for making governmental regulation effective, and faith that litigation will remedy injustices.

The Merits of the Adversary System

The adversary system has severe critics; it is also lauded as a vital protection of American democracy and freedom. Comparison of the adversary system with the judge-centered procedure of other legal systems, however, often posits an idealization of one against the realities of the other. A balanced analysis requires recognition of realities in both systems, and of the fact that litigation is inherently contentious and ridden with uncertainty.

The criticisms of the adversary system are essentially threefold: the system nurtures rabid partisanship; it distorts the search for justice into a "game of wits"; and it gives unfair advantage to affluent litigants and "repeat players," the latter term referring to businesses that are frequently involved in litigation. While these criticisms all have merit, in varying measure they also apply to the civil law system.

There is no question that the adversary system invites and requires partisanship. Indeed, that is the system's very design. Yet it is difficult to believe that litigants would behave otherwise in the individualistic and competitive American culture, with its moralistic sentiments and its legalistic politics. Similar partisanship is manifested in nonjudicial proceedings in this country—for example, hearings of school boards and zoning boards, legislative hearings, news conferences, protest demonstrations, and election campaigns. Except in small towns, modern American culture places low value on group solidarity, deference to the feelings of others, compromise, and mutual forbearance. If social values such as deference to the feelings of others were highly valued, one would expect them to be manifested in American litigation, and indeed to see litigation as a last resort for conflict resolution. However, America does not have such a culture. Party partisanship in litigation is of a piece with the peculiar American attribute that combines aversion to constituted authority with deep commitment to the ideal of law. The adversary system of litigation thus is a convenient target for those who are offended by more deeply imbedded characteristics of American culture.

A related criticism of the adversary system concerns the partisanship of lawyers. It is contended that American advocates magnify their clients' partisanship. This is often true of courtroom behavior, where many American lawyers behave as boors, not having been tutored in how to be tough and polite at the same time. However, more subtle analysis of the advocate's partisanship is required.

In the first place, the advocate's partisanship in the adversary system is salient because the advocate's role is salient. Advocates in other legal systems are equally partisan, but they must mask their partisanship in the cloak of deference to the judge. Moreover, the American advocate's belligerence is often designed to sustain the client's courage in the ordeal of litigation, litigation being an ordeal whatever the procedural system. A psychologically strong front must be maintained in litigation for the same reason it is maintained by diplomats in international confrontations.

In any event, a competent advocate, whatever the procedural system, is also a detached judge of the client's cause. Detachment is required for accurately evaluating the claim or defense at the outset and for reevaluating it as the litigation proceeds. Such a mentality is especially necessary in settling a case, when the litigants must be extricated from their partisan passions. More than 90 percent of civil litigation in the American adversary system is settled before trial.

The criticism that the adversary system converts litigation into a "game" is simply naive: litigation is a "game" whatever procedural system is employed. As technically defined, a game is a transaction involving stakes whose allocation depends on interaction of the participants under conditions of uncertainty. Litigation precisely fits this definition; indeed, the classic "prisoner's dilemma" of game theory revolves around a problem of criminal litigation. In a similar vein, the adversary system is criticized because it gives the advocates incentive to keep the tribunal from learning about adverse evidence, if that can be done within the rules. But such is also the incentive of the advocates in the judge-centered procedure of the civil law. The difference between the two systems is in the rules of the game, not in whether a game is involved.

From the viewpoint of the court, of course, litigation is a different kind of game. The court is not interested in winning, but in determining who should win. In pursuing this objective, however, the court has its own stratagems. For example, when a judge becomes convinced that one side ought to prevail on the merits, he may extend every procedural advantage to the other side, so that the losing party cannot complain of unfairness after losing. These and other judicial "games" are exhibited in all procedural systems.

The third objection to the adversary system is that it favors the rich against the poor. In general this is true. The adversary system depends on effective advocacy; advocates differ in their ability; and effective advocates can more readily be retained by paying a higher fee. However, the same differentials exist in proceedings that do not use the adversary system, for example, legal representation in American legislative hearings and administrative rule-making proceedings and in the civil law system of adjudication. The underlying reality is that where the legal profession is not a monopoly of the state, there is a market for legal services. In any market, those who are able to pay higher prices are able to gain better resources for themselves.

The more serious question, therefore, is whether the structure of a procedural system provides a compensating balance between parties who are not equally represented. The fairness of the adversary system, by its very structure, requires adequate legal representation of both parties. The American system has generally failed to meet this requirement, for provision of legal aid to indigent civil litigants is grossly inadequate. That being so, the American courts should more fully employ other counterbalancing procedures. In cases involving indigents, the role of the judge should be made more central, as in the civil law system: the judge should assist the development and presentation of an unrepresented party's case and help question the witnesses and articulate the applicable law. American judges in fact often do this, but unsystematically, because the court's procedure, staff, and definition of its responsibilities are not equipped for the task.

More fundamentally, judicial intervention to counterbalance the abilities of the parties would contradict American political premises. It would constitute activist benevolence on the part of governmental authority, which is regarded as suspect by many segments of American public opinion. The civil law pattern can be seen as inconsistent with the principle of party autonomy, which echoes the American ideals of personal liberty and equality. Paradoxically, some of the harshest American critics of the adversary system are also critics of constituted authority of any kind, including judicial authority.

In any event, it must be asked whether other legal systems in practice fulfill their obligations to equal treatment of parties in civil justice. The record of experience indicates that the civil law system is little better than the adversary system in this respect. The civil law system depends upon a judiciary that has the time, the supporting staff, and the will to develop each contested case in a full and balanced way. In most countries the resources to accomplish these purposes are grossly inadequate. Court calendars are overburdened, the judges have no pretrial investigators to search out evidence, nor staff to document the issues and the applicable law. When civil law judges take extra time in an unexpectedly complicated case, their schedule for other cases is disrupted. Those acquainted with caseloads in American welfare and unemployment agencies would recognize a similar pattern.

The adversary system operates reasonably satisfactorily where both parties have the resources to obtain competent advocates. The judge-centered civil law system operates reasonably satisfactorily where the judiciary has adequate resources to perform its function. Generally speaking, the poor are ill-served in both systems.

CHAPTER SIX

The Pretrial Stage

A civil action is commenced by plaintiff's filing of a complaint with the court. Thereupon, a summons to opposing parties is issued, directing them to respond to the complaint or suffer a judgment by default. A copy of the complaint must be attached to the summons, thus notifying the defendant of the terms of the claim. The defendant has a specified period of time in which to respond, usually thirty days.

The complaint must be a concise narrative of the plaintiff's grievance, alleging facts which enable the court to award judgment for plaintiff, if the facts alleged are proved. The narrative statements are called allegations, and are usually organized as follows: first, identification of the plaintiff and the defendant; second, description of the transaction in which they were involved; third, description of the conduct of the defendant that produced injury to the plaintiff; fourth, statement of the nature and extent of plaintiff's damages resulting from the injury; and, finally, a demand for judgment. The demand is often called the "prayer for relief" because in premodern times the plaintiff was a supplicant for official dispensation. In federal court the plaintiff must also allege the basis of the court's jurisdiction over the subject matter of the dispute—for example, that the claim arises under federal law or because the parties are of diverse citizenship.

The facts are presented in terms that reflect the legal theory upon which the complaint is based. They form the basis for preliminary consideration of the complaint's legal validity and will constitute the factual foundation for the trial.

A complaint in a simple motor vehicle accident may be no more than two or three pages long. Its allegations would be substantially as follows:

I. Plaintiff John Miller was crossing Chapel Street, New Haven, Connecticut, on July 31, 1992. Plaintiff used the pedestrian crosswalk at College Street in doing so.

II. Defendant Michael Smith is the owner and operator of a Ford automobile. On July 31, 1992, defendant drove that car along Chapel Street. Defendant failed to keep control of the car and failed to keep watch for pedestrians.

III. As a proximate result of defendant's failure as alleged, defendant's car struck and injured plaintiff.

IV. As a further proximate result, plaintiff has suffered permanent bodily injury, pain, and distress, and has incurred medical expenses and lost wages.

Wherefore, plaintiff prays judgment for $75,000 damages.

A complaint in a complicated financial case involving multiple transactions and multiple parties can be one hundred pages or even longer. In claims based on contracts or other documentation, copies of the documents are attached to the complaint as exhibits. When a claim is based on a statute, it is customary to recite the statute.

The defendant's response to the factual allegations is made in an answer, which is a counternarrative. Uncontested facts will be admitted, for example, the identity of the parties in most cases. Contested allegations will be denied, thus creating issues of fact. For example, the defendant's answer to the complaint described above would likely be as follows:

Answering plaintiff's complaint, defendant:

I. Admits that plaintiff was on or about Chapel Street, New Haven, Connecticut, on July 31, 1992.

II. Admits that defendant is the owner of a Ford automobile

and that the vehicle was involved in an accident on July 31, 1992.

III. Except as admitted above, denies the allegations of the complaint.

The issues of fact in the case can be ascertained by comparing the pleadings. If the defendant has affirmative defenses, they are pleaded as additional narrative. For example, the defendant may contend that plaintiff had opportunity to mitigate damages and hence has no right to impose liability on the defendant. Such an allegation by the defendant would create another issue of fact.

At the early stages of the case, the pleadings set forth the parties' maximum contentions as they are then comprehended. As discovery progresses, evidence may reveal that certain allegations cannot be proven or that additional allegations are warranted, or that there should be joinder of additional parties whose interests are involved. These developments thereafter are addressed through amendments to the pleadings, whereby allegations may be withdrawn or added. Under modern American procedure, amendments are liberally allowed, particularly where they reflect new information revealed in pretrial discovery. The pleadings therefore present the factual issues for determination at trial, adjusted in light of information produced through discovery.

The pleadings also present legal issues. Implicit in a legally valid complaint is the premise that the facts, if proved, entitle plaintiff to judgment. The illustrative complaint above, for example, implicitly contends that if a person suffers bodily injury as a result of another's failure to exercise reasonable care, then the injured party is entitled to judgment for compensatory damages. The legal issue in such a case is simple and obvious, and indeed will not be disputed. Rather, if the case goes to trial, it will be on the factual issue of whether defendant was at fault.

However, many cases involve disputes over legal issues. A legal issue is always involved when a party asserts a novel legal theory, as in *Brown v. Board of Education*. The plaintiff's legal theory was that as a matter of constitutional law a child's race could not be used as a basis for assigning the child to a public school. The facts in that case were not disputed; rather, it was a "test case" seeking a determination, eventually from the appellate courts, that school segregation was inconsistent with the Equal Projection Clause of the Constitution.

Issues of fact are resolved on the basis of evidence presented at trial. Issues of law may be resolved in advance of trial. Pretrial resolution of an issue of law can be precipitated if the defendant asks the court to dismiss the claim as lacking a legally sufficient basis. The court then refers to the pleadings and, for purposes of deciding the legal issue, assumes that the allegations of the complaint are true. On this assumption, the court can then determine the legal issue. If the court determines that the claim, if proved, is legally valid, then the case proceeds to trial. If the court determines that the claim, even if proved, is legally invalid, then the action is dismissed at the pleading stage. Plaintiff may then appeal, seeking review of the trial court's determination of the legal issue.

The court has authority to question the legal validity of a complaint or of an affirmative defense on its own initiative. However, a court rarely exercises such authority, but will assume that if there is such an issue, the opposing party will raise it.

It should be evident from the foregoing analysis that the pleadings define the issues presented in a legal dispute. For this reason they can be the vehicle by which very important legal issues are decided, first by the trial court and then by an appellate court. For example, plaintiff's allegations could state that as an employee she was discharged without her employer having given reasons. These allegations imply the novel legal theory that an employer must give reasons in discharging an employee, whereas traditionally an employer could discharge an employee without reason, so long as there was no violation of restrictions such as those against gender, race, and age discrimination. To confront a complaint with these allegations, the defendant employer would no doubt move to dismiss on the ground that, as a matter of law, plaintiff had no case.

Plaintiff's counterargument would be that the law governing the employment relationship should afford an employee this new protection. In deciding whether to dismiss the action, the trial court would have to resolve the argument over what the law governing employment should be. If the court dismisses the plaintiff's claim, plaintiff could carry the argument to the appellate courts.

At one level of analysis, the ruling in the hypothetical-employee case resolved a "technical" question of procedure: Was the complaint sufficient to permit the action to proceed? Indeed, the ruling did resolve that question. But through the mechanism of that technical ruling, the court also decided a very important question of employment law.

A more general point is that many "technical" rulings on procedure are the occasion for deciding crucial issues of law, and with them issues of social policy. Indeed, it is often difficult to comprehend what a court has decided in a substantive issue except by understanding the procedural context of the court's decision. Sir Henry Maine, a great scholar of legal history, observed that under ancient law, substantive law was "secreted in the interstices of procedure."[1] That observation holds in modern procedure as well.

Pretrial Motions

The stage between the commencement of the action with the complaint and the completion of discovery is called the pretrial stage. As explained in the next section, discovery involves each party's obtaining testimony, documents, and other evidence from opposing parties in advance of trial. Thereafter, the trial will be held, if the case has not been settled.

During the pretrial stage there may be motions addressing various legal problems in the case. A motion is a request by a party that the court take specified action. Motions during trial ordinarily are made orally; pretrial motions ordinarily are made in writing, with documentation that includes a memorandum of law arguing the legal grounds supporting the motion. If facts must be established as a basis for the motion, they are usually presented by written affidavit. If the motion is contested, the objection will be expressed in an opposition memorandum of legal argument, with affidavits if additional facts are relevant. The court will hear oral argument and decide the issue. The form of a motion might be, for example:

Plaintiff moves the court for permission to join as an additional Defendant the XYZ Corporation. Evidence revealed in discovery, as more fully set forth in the affidavit attached hereto, shows that the driver of the vehicle involved in the accident was an employee of XYZ Corporation and was engaged in this employment at the time of the accident. Accordingly, XYZ Corporation as well as the Defendant driver may be liable for Plaintiff's injuries.

As the foregoing example indicates, pretrial motions often emanate from the discovery process, but motions can address almost any substantive or procedural aspect of the case. Typical pretrial motions may address the following problems: the court's competence and proper venue; the scope of the litigation; pretrial procedure itself; or the merits of the case.

A motion concerning the court's competence is made by the defendant, except in the extraordinary circumstance where a plaintiff, having selected the court, concludes that the court lacks competence. A challenge to the court's competence is usually made immediately after the complaint is filed, because the lack of competence ordinarily will be evident at that point. For example, if the court's competence is limited in terms of the amount involved in the litigation, defendant may show by affidavit that the amount recoverable by plaintiff could not come within those monetary limits. In a federal court action based on diversity of citizenship, the defendant may have facts showing that the plaintiff and the defendant are actually citizens of the same state, and hence that the federal court lacks diversity jurisdiction.

Generally speaking, a state court may exercise its judicial authority over transactions that occur wholly or substantially within its borders, but it may not exercise authority over persons who have no connection to the state. This dimension of state court authority is called the state's territorial jurisdiction and evolves from the independent legal status of the states in the American federation, discussed in chapter 2. A problem similar to lack of diversity jurisdiction in federal court may arise in state court litigation involving events that transpired in more than one state, or when a resident of one state was involved in a transaction in another state.

Similar to the objection concerning territorial jurisdiction is objection to venue. Venue refers to the geographical location of the trial court. In state courts, the rules of venue determine the county within the state in which the action may properly be brought. In federal courts, the rules of venue determine the federal district in which the action may properly be brought. In general, actions may be brought in the place where the transaction arose or in which the defendant resides. Some types of litigation are governed by special venue rules; for example, actions concerning real property must usually be brought where the land is located. Objection to improper venue must be made by motion submitted immediately after the complaint is filed, or the objection is waived.

Motions concerning the scope of the litigation may be made by either party. Matters addressed in such motions include: adding persons as plaintiffs or defendants because they have an interest in the dispute that was not previously perceived; eliminating parties who have been improperly joined, when it appears they have no interest in the dispute; adding claims or legal theories, suggested by evidence produced in discovery or by change in circumstances; or eliminating claims or legal theories because it has become clear that there is no evidence to support them. Often there will be no objection to such a motion. Motions concerning procedure may be made by either party. Typically, the motion objects that the opposing party is doing something improper or is improperly refusing to honor its duty under the procedural rules. Many pretrial motions concern discovery, asserting, for example, that responses to discovery demands have not been made, or are incomplete, or are tardy;

that the discovery demands are too burdensome or too vague or seek privileged material; or that the opposing party refuses to attend a scheduled deposition. Motions may complain that opposing counsel is guilty of misconduct—for example, that access to evidence is being obstructed, or that counsel has an improper conflict of interest. A motion may complain about the conduct of the judge, asserting, for example, that the judge should disqualify himself because of interest in the case or familiarity with the transaction involved. The procedure for such motions is generally the same as that described above.

Finally, motions may be addressed to the merits of the case. Of these, the most important are the motion to dismiss for failure to state a claim or for judgment on the pleadings, and the motion for summary judgment.

The motion to dismiss for failure to state a claim attacks the substantive validity of the claim stated in the complaint. The motion involves a contention by defendant as follows: Assuming for purposes of argument that the facts in the complaint are true (without admitting them for other purposes), plaintiff is not entitled to judgment because those facts involve no legal wrong.

Thus, suppose plaintiff, a well-known public figure, sues a newspaper for defamation, alleging a defamatory account but not alleging that the newspaper management knew the statement was false or was recklessly indifferent to its falsity. Defendant could move to dismiss on the ground that, under the American law of defamation, a newspaper cannot be held liable for a false news story about a public figure unless it knew the story was false or was reckless regarding the truth of the story.[2] The motion would assume, implicitly and hypothetically, that the story was defamatory, but would contend that liability also requires knowledge or recklessness, which have not been alleged. The defendant's motion to dismiss for failure to state a claim poses an issue of law. If the issue is resolved in defendant's favor, that resolution terminates the litigation. There would be neither discovery nor a trial, for both would be unnecessary if the motion is granted. Of course, the motion will be denied if the judge disagrees with defendant's argument about the legal merit of plaintiff's claim. In that event, discovery proceeds and trial may be required.

In this way a motion to dismiss for failure to state a claim can determine a case at the pretrial stage. A similar procedure, called a general demurrer, was available to defendant at common law and under code pleading.

The motion for judgment on the pleadings has a similar logic. Such a motion may be made by the defendant after filing an answer to the complaint. A plaintiff may make a similar motion to contest the legal validity of an affirmative defense asserted in a defendant's answer. For example, the defendant may have pleaded the statute of limitations, on the premise that the time period applicable to the plaintiff's claim is one year. The plaintiff contends that the applicable time period is two years, that the action was brought within that period, and therefore that the statute of limitations defense is legally untenable. The plaintiff's contention may be asserted by a motion to strike out the limitations defense from the defendant's answer. Such a motion creates an issue of law for the court concerning the proper limitations period to be applied.

Another pretrial motion commonly employed concerning the substantive merits of a case is the motion for summary judgment.

As its name implies, the motion requests immediate judgment for the moving party without having a trial. The motion contends that the evidence clearly establishes the facts and that the moving party is entitled to judgment on those facts. In support of the motion, evidence obtained in discovery can be used, as well as affidavits. The logic underlying summary judgment is the same as that underlying the motion to dismiss, except that the factual basis of a summary judgment motion is evidence rather than the complaint's allegations.

For example, suppose in a newspaper defamation case the plaintiff has alleged that defendant acted recklessly, but defendant develops through discovery the following facts: plaintiff in his deposition admits that he has no personal knowledge about the investigation made by the newspaper before publishing the story; the newspaper person who wrote the story in her deposition describes the sources she consulted, which included the police, old newspaper files, and several people acquainted with the plaintiff; and the newspaper editor in his deposition describes newspaper's standard fact-checking procedure and states that it was used in preparing the present story. Defendant retains as an expert a news media person not associated with defendant, who gives an affidavit that the fact-checking procedures used in the case are recognized standards in the newspaper industry.

On the basis of this evidence, defendant moves for summary judgment, attaching the affidavit and the deposition transcripts as supporting material. Defendant's legal argument is as follows: Defendant is liable only if it knew the story was false or acted recklessly in publishing it; there is no evidence defendant knew the story was false; there is positive evidence that defendant used reasonable care in checking the story, and use of such care excludes recklessness; therefore, it is indisputable that an essential condition of liability does not exist; therefore, defendant is entitled to have judgment summarily entered in its favor.

This example demonstrates how discovery can be used not only to prepare for trial but to obtain evidence that precludes a trial. Discovery and motion procedure can similarly be used to narrow the claims and defenses by eliminating their legally untenable components. Discovery also provides the parties a basis for more accurately assessing their chances of success at trial. In this respect, discovery is a settlement procedure.

Scope and Mechanics of Discovery

Once action is commenced, the parties are empowered to take discovery against each other. Discovery demands are initiated by the parties, without a requirement of prior approval of the court. Thus, if plaintiff wishes to interrogate the defendant in a deposition before trial, plaintiff simply gives written notice to defendant's advocate specifying a time and place for the deposition. Similarly, a party wishing to discover documents in possession of an opposing party simply makes a written demand identifying the type of documents to be produced.

The discovery process as a whole proceeds through the initiative of the advocates, through demand and response. Depositions are taken in the presence of a court reporter but ordinarily without the presence of a judge or other judicial official. Documents discovery proceeds in the same way. Disputes over the propriety of discovery endeavors are usually worked out through negotiation. However, a ruling may be requested from the court where the dispute cannot be resolved in this way. Discovery disputes may be determined by a judge or assistant judge specially assigned to that responsibility, or by the judge to whom the case is assigned for trial.

Discovery has broad scope. According to Federal Rule 26, which is the model in modern procedural codes, inquiry made be made into "any matter, not privileged, that is relevant to the subject matter of the action." Thus, discovery may be had of facts incidentally relevant to the issues in the pleadings even if the facts do not directly prove or disprove the facts in question. For example, in a personal injury case, defendant may inquire whether plaintiff has previously suffered injuries, for that may be relevant in determining the severity of the injuries that occurred in the immediate accident.

Only three objections are effective against a discovery request: one, that it seeks material which is completely irrelevant; two, that the request is unfairly burdensome, but only if the burden is very severe or if the information can be supplied in some other way; three, if the request seeks privileged information.

There are several privileges, the principal ones being as follows:

The privilege against self-incrimination, allowing refusal to give an answer that would tend to incriminate the person responding. This privilege is available in civil as well as criminal cases, and may be claimed by a party or by a third-person witness.

The attorney-client privilege, allowing refusal to disclose

confidential communications between client and attorney. This privilege covers a nonparty's communications with its attorney as well as those between a party and the party's attorney.

The lawyer's work-product privilege, or "work-product immunity." This privilege allows refusal to disclose memoranda written by the lawyer or by the party in preparing for litigation. For example, the lawyer's notes of interviews with witnesses are immune from discovery by the other party, except in extraordinary circumstances.

The physician-patient privilege, allowing refusal to disclose communications in the course of treatment between a patient and a physician. However, the privilege is inapplicable when a litigant puts his or her own bodily condition in issue, as occurs in a suit for personal injuries.

Several other privileges are invoked less frequently. In the case of the federal government, a national security ("state secrets") privilege is recognized. Some states confer a privilege on communications between financial accountant and client. There is also a priest-penitent privilege, but it rarely is involved in civil litigation. Because the scope of discovery is so broad, the shelter of privilege is urgently sought when it is available. Disputes arising in discovery have generated complex decisional law concerning privilege.

The mechanisms for conducting discovery are of four types:

deposition, which is elicitation and verbatim recording of a witness's testimony by questioning under oath;
inspection of documents and other things in possession of an opposing party or third person;
physical or mental examination of a person whose bodily condition is in issue; and
demands for admission.

Deposition and document inspection are the mechanisms most often used, and are considered in chapter 5. The analysis there applies in general to the other discovery mechanisms.

Physical examination is obtained as a matter of course in personal injury cases. The procedure requires that the plaintiff submit to a private professional examination by an expert, usually a medical doctor, retained by the defendant. The examiner must give plaintiff a copy of his report, and the plaintiff then is required to supply defendant with all prior medical history of the same condition. In practice, the procedure is routine.

Demands for admission permit a party to propound proposed statements of fact to the opposing party and demand that the statements be admitted as true. Admissions obtained in response are conclusive in the immediate litigation, but are not admissible elsewhere. If a party refuses to make the admission, and the interrogating party proves the facts at trial, the costs of making the proof are awarded. The mechanism is useful with respect to facts that are not really disputable but require complicated evidence.

Discovery serves two important legitimate purposes. It permits each side to probe the other side's evidence and it permits each side to obtain evidence that may help prove its case. By way of exploring the other side's evidence, for example, testimony of the principal witnesses for the opposition, including the opposing party, may be taken in a pretrial deposition. The witness is subjected to a cross-examination concerning his or her memory of the matters involved in the dispute. By way of obtaining evidence to prove the party's own case, for example, documents in the possession of the opposing litigant or a third party must be produced for inspection and copying at the pretrial stage and thus may reveal facts advantageous to the discovering party. The results produced in discovery can be used in trial. For example, statements from a witness's deposition may be used in cross-examination at trial, to test for inconsistencies in the witness's testimony. So also, documents obtained in discovery may be introduced as evidence at trial. For example, medical records of a personal injury claimant, obtained in discovery, can be used to prove that the plaintiff was in disabled condition before the immediate accident occurred.

Discovery also can be used for the illegitimate purpose of inflicting delay and expense on the opposing party. For example, a deposition of the opposing party can be protracted through repetitive or irrelevant questioning and can be carried out in a psychologically oppressive manner. Similarly, a request for documents can be so broad as to impose a serious burden of cost and inconvenience, requiring a business to search through files going back over many years. In many cases, no clear distinction can be drawn between discovery that is thorough although aggressive and discovery that is unnecessary and abusive. Abuse of discovery can be penalized by the court, but in practice only flagrant abuse will be addressed. As a result the parties must be self-protective; retaliation by responsive abuse is the usual weapon.

Depositions and Production of Documents

A discovery deposition is taken upon written demand by the discovering party, court permission ordinarily not being required. The demand specifies the time and place for the deposition, usually in the law office of the advocate representing the party with whom the witness is associated; neutral witnesses usually are examined at the office of the discovering advocate. All questions and answers are recorded and reproduced in a typed transcript. The questioning usually is detailed and aggressive. A deposition of three to five hours is not unusual, leading to a transcript of hundreds of pages. Some depositions require several days, even weeks. Depositions of all principal witnesses will be taken, including parties and officials of corporate parties, and those of all significant independent witnesses. Where documents are involved in the underlying transaction, the witness will be examined in detail about them.

Disputes often arise during depositions. Ordinarily no judicial officer is at hand to resolve them immediately. The advocates then either resolve the dispute by agreement, often grudgingly, or reserve the dispute for later resolution by the court. Sometimes the party objecting to the questioning—for example, on the ground that it seeks privileged information—will instruct the witness not to answer. In extreme cases the objecting party will discontinue the deposition, leaving the dispute to be negotiated later or submitted to the court.

Documents production also begins by demand of the discovering party. The demand describes the types of documents sought, and the responding party is required to produce all documents in its possession that fall within the description. To preclude evasion, the discovering party's demand is intricately detailed and sweepingly comprehensive. The responding party may object to the breadth of the request but must produce documents relevant to the controversy.

Production of documents in major litigation can yield literally tens of thousands of documents. The task of correlating this information is itself a science. Specialized computer programs can access the full text of documents and facilitate retrieval by various categories. A full-time documents archivist is often required. In multiparty cases where documents are produced for many sources, a common documents repository may be established.

Discovery in many cases is enveloped in mistrust and fear of cheating, especially where the stakes are high. There is strong temptation to cheat. An advocate may subtly suggest that the client destroy or misplace relevant documents, or by casuistical interpretation may conclude that inculpating documents are not within the scope of the demand. In these days when multiple copies are made of many documents, however, the risk of being caught is significant. Cheating in discovery, if proven, can result in severe sanctions. The innocent party's expenses in uncovering the misconduct can be awarded; key issues in the case can be deemed resolved against the offending party; in extreme cases, the whole cost of the litigation can be charged against the offending party and adverse judgment entered without trial. However, cases where cheating has been found are infrequent.

Less dramatic violations of the discovery rules are more frequent. Excessively broad demands for production of documents can be limited by a responsive ruling of the court. Harassment in deposition may be limited by similar ruling. If the discovery process becomes embittered, a special judicial officer may be appointed as referee. The court is also empowered to impose monetary sanctions for abuse of discovery, including attorneys' fees unnecessarily incurred by the victimized party.

In most cases discovery proceeds without incident. Various levels of contentiousness become standard in different practice settings. For example, discovery in small-town litigation, or between lawyers who regularly are involved with each other, usually is very casual. Discovery in large-scale litigation by national law firms is usually done strictly according to the rules, often with much conflict over their interpretation.

Discovery of Expert Testimony

Use of experts is ubiquitous except in cases involving very simple issues, such as nonpayment of a debt. In personal injury cases, both parties will have medical experts to address the nature of the injury and the extent of rehabilitation; where the plaintiff has had large income-earning capacity, or is a housewife who has little monetary income, compensation experts may address the measure of economic loss; in automobile accidents, accident diagnosticians may interpret the circumstances (skid marks, configuration of the impact, and so forth) to give an opinion about how the accident occurred. Accounting experts will be employed in business and financial cases, soil experts in environmental cases, economic analysts in antitrust cases, fellow professionals in malpractice cases, construction engineers in building contract cases, and so on. More than one expert may be employed on a case, sometimes many experts on various subjects.

Expert testimony is especially sensitive in two respects. First, an expert may function not only as a witness, which is the expert's formal role, but also as a protagonist not unlike an advocate. Experts used as trial witnesses are selected both for their technical competence and for their skill and effectiveness in presenting opinions. The trier of fact, especially if it is a jury, may be as impressed with the clarity and directness of an expert's testimony as with his credentials. The outcome of many cases can depend on the expert witnesses.

Second, an expert in analyzing the specific problem in his domain will ordinarily become familiar with the legal strategy of the party retaining him. Accordingly, having retained an expert, a party will wish to keep tight control on contact between the expert and opposing parties. An additional problem arises when an expert provides an adverse opinion, a fact that the party retaining the expert does not want revealed.

The policy of the discovery rules concerning experts is very protective of the parties' interests, as against the interest of making experts freely available to give their opinions. If a party employs an expert for preliminary consultation, disclosure of the expert's identity is not required, nor is his opinion. If a party employs an expert who gives an opinion that the party wishes to use at trial, however, then the identity of the expert and the substance of his or her opinions may be discovered by opposing parties. A party may not employ an expert previously employed by another party in the same litigation, without the latter's consent. Thus, a party may be able to use a favorable expert opinion and to "bury" an unfavorable one.

The rules do not give a right to examine the opposing party's trial expert by deposition except upon special order of the court. However, by general practice the parties stipulate for reciprocal depositions of experts. The parties thus can estimate how forceful the respective experts will be at trial, and evaluate settlement prospects accordingly.

Pretrial Conference

In complicated cases, there will be a pretrial conference after discovery is completed and before trial. The conference is conducted by the judge with the advocates and its purpose is to specify the issues to be tried, as revealed by discovery. The order entered in this conference, called the pretrial order, also may specify the witnesses to be called by each side at trial and the documentary proof to be received. The pretrial order supersedes the pleadings and governs the conduct of the trial. Issues and evidence other than those specified in the pretrial order will not be considered at trial except in extraordinary circumstances. A pretrial conference is a regular procedure in federal courts, but many state courts hold pretrial conferences only in complex cases. In such cases the court may conduct a series of pretrial conferences, beginning soon after the complaint is filed, continuing through the pretrial stage, and dealing with all kinds of substantive legal questions, discovery controversies, and other procedural matters. Assistant judicial officers may be employed to supervise discovery. In effect the court may become an administrative manager for the case. Intensive involvement of the court has been criticized as somehow invasive of the parties' procedural rights, but is generally accepted as necessary to the orderly conduct of cases involving multiple parties and issues. It may also be noted that such a role for the court is ordinary practice in most other legal systems.

Settlement Procedures

Generally speaking, parties to civil litigation have autonomy to conclude the dispute by a contract of settlement. In certain cases, court approval is required—for example, claims of a minor or a legally incapacitated person, claims by certain fiduciaries, and class action claims. Otherwise, the court accepts the settlement without examining its fairness, which is considered a matter for the parties to determine.

A settlement typically is a compromise in which the plaintiff receives less than his demand. However, a settlement may call for no payment or full payment. A settlement with no payment might be agreed where, for example, the court has ruled against a plaintiff's novel legal theory and the plaintiff does not want to incur the expense of an appeal. A settlement for full payment might be agreed where, for example, discovery evidence indicates that defendant has no defense to the claim. Settlement allows the parties to avoid further litigation expense and usually provides that neither side shall recover costs or incidental expenses from the other. A settlement may be reached at any time—before discovery has commenced, during discovery or at the pretrial conference, during trial, or even after trial and before an appeal is completed.

Negotiation between the advocates is the primary mechanism of settlement. Experienced advocates are generally expert at evaluating cases and skilled in settlement negotiation. However, many courts have procedures to facilitate settlement. One procedure is the settlement conference at which a judge presides, seeking to encourage flexibility in positions and providing an impartial estimate of a reasonable compromise. The parties themselves may be required to attend such a conference, especially when they appear to be stubborn about compromise. The judge may exercise persuasive influence, sometimes amounting to strong pressure, but may not impose a settlement. Some such procedures require that a judge who presides at settlement conference may not preside at the trial.

In some states there is also a procedure called settlement offer. Under this procedure, a party may at the pretrial stage make a firm written offer of settlement in a stated amount. If the offer is accepted by the opposing party, settlement results. If not, the party refusing the settlement must pay the offering party's costs of continuing the litigation, including attorneys' fees, unless the refusing party obtains a better result in the trial. Since attorneys' fees ordinarily are not recovered by the prevailing party, this procedure is a strong settlement incentive.

Various additional procedures, generally known as "alternative dispute resolution," can be used.[3] One of these procedure calls for a mediator to seek a negotiated settlement. Another calls for a "minitrial"—a short mock trial of the case at which the parties present their principal witnesses and then discuss settlement in light of the performance. Where witness credibility is important, a mock jury may be used as well, to give a hypothetical verdict and to discuss the jurors' impressions of the evidence, upon the basis of which the parties can discuss settlement. The purpose of such procedures is to enable the parties and their advocates to assess the case more realistically, and thereby to become better disposed to compromise. There are also procedures for arbitrating certain types of cases, particularly those involving limited monetary claims. The procedure may be optional, but in many cases it is compulsory. The arbitration consists of an expedited trial before a tribunal of three neutral lawyers or judicial referees. If the arbitration award is accepted, that resolves the case. If a party rejects the award, then regular trial ensues, but the party rejecting the award must pay the cost of the arbitration if that party does not obtain a better result in the trial.

Arbitration is also used when the parties have previously agreed to that procedure. Arbitration agreements are almost universally employed in building contracts and are widely employed in commercial transactions.

Comparison with Civil Law First-Instance Proceedings

The structure and sequence of litigation in American procedure is quite different from its civil law counterpart. The principal differences are as follows:

In the American system, the advocates formulate the legal theories for the case and the judge simply chooses among them. In the civil law system, the judge formulates the legal theories for the case, sometimes adopting but often ignoring the parties' legal arguments.

In the American adversary system, the advocates control the development and presentation of the case; in the civil law system, the judge is responsible—at least theoretically—for the case and the advocates merely make supplemental suggestions.

The American system involves elaborate, often extended pretrial exploration of evidence, followed by a short, concentrated trial. In the civil law system, no distinction is made between pretrial and trial. Rather, the trial has a preliminary stage in which the issues are identified and documentary evidence received, followed, if necessary, by a hearing. Civil law systems do not employ any form of pretrial discovery of evidence. In the preliminary hearing, evidence is not "discovered"; the parties apply for submission of items of evidence and the judge delivers rulings about the relevance and admissibility of the evidence. Admissible evidence will be presented, for the first and only time, in the ensuing trial hearings.

In the American system, the judgment after trial in the first-instance court is subject to appeal regarding legal issues, but with very limited scope of review concerning factual issues. In the civil law system, the judgment of the first-instance court is subject to comprehensive reconsideration in the court of second instance, which is responsible for the justness of the result in terms of both law and fact.

Particularly distinctive in the American system are the largely unsupervised control by the advocates over the pretrial development of the evidence, and the use of a jury in the trial of damages cases. Particularly distinctive in the civil law system is the court's authority to formulate its own legal theory of the case and to develop and determine the facts as well.

However, these distinctions are balanced by important functional similarities. The American system in operation has many characteristics of the civil law system, and vice versa. The control exercised by American advocates in the pretrial phase is diminished because the advocates work at cross-purposes and thereby neutralize each other's efforts. The resulting deadlocks must be referred to the court, which then can exercise control not unlike its civil law counterpart. So also, the control the advocates have over legal theories can be superseded by the court. For example, the court may exclude entire categories of discovery on the ground that the issues to which they relate are legally irrelevant, or enlarge the case by interjecting new legal theories. In appellate review in the American system, the court is nominally limited to issues of law, but that court has final authority to define whether an issue is one of law rather than of fact. It is a frequent complaint of American trial judges that the appellate courts too often succumb to the temptation to "retry the case" in the guise of reviewing for error.

Considering the civil law system, the control exercised by the first-instance judge is often more formal than real. Busy judges often simply follow the lead suggested by the advocates concerning the issues, the evidence, and the appropriate legal theories. Judges often produce confusion because they have not fully comprehended the issues, leaving a judgment vulnerable to revision by the second-instance court, which also provides the advocates a second opportunity to retry the case before a different panel of judges.

Discovery in International Litigation

The central role of party-initiated pretrial discovery in American procedure often creates legal policy conflicts in litigation of international transactions in American courts. These conflicts are especially intense when the underlying legal claims are incompatible with the legal policy of the other country involved. Treaty provisions moderate the conflict, but American courts nevertheless tend to give precedence to American procedure.

American discovery rules allow a special latitude that is unknown in the procedures of other countries: that of compelling the opposing party to produce documents. Production of confidential business documents is especially controversial. The American procedural law compels their production at party initiative, while the law of most other countries makes their production exceptional, and then only upon court order.

This conflict in procedural policy is exacerbated by substantive policy differences in certain fields, such as antitrust law. American antitrust law is traditionally hostile to market-sharing agreements between businesses in the same industry, whereas European law until recent years encouraged market sharing, as does the law of many other countries today. There has been similarly sharp difference in the law governing liability of manufacturers of products that have caused personal injury, and in the law governing banking and securities transactions. American courts usually apply the American liability rules, which tend to be much more favorable to the claimant. As a result, not only do foreign defendants object, but their governments often do so at the diplomatic level as well.

The Hague Convention, adopted in 1970, sought to resolve these conflicts. The convention's provisions give precedence to the country in which the documents are located to determine whether and by what procedure they must be produced. The procedure specified in the convention is cumbersome and ordinarily results in much more limited discovery than allowed under American law. Foreign defendants in American litigation have contended that the Hague Convention should control, but the U.S. Supreme Court has held that it does not control if its terms would unfairly inhibit discovery.[4] Since the convention procedure is almost always more restrictive than American civil procedure, and most lower court judges consider such restrictions unfair, the lower courts usually allow use of the American discovery rules.

CHAPTER SEVEN

The Trial

The most conspicuous characteristic of American civil procedure is the jury system. No other legal system employs juries as the norm in civil cases, although in many of the civil law systems there are nonlawyer members of certain specialized courts, particularly ones having competence in labor matters. However, even in these tribunals the lay person is selected on the basis of experience in the subject matter or as the representative of a concerned interest group. Moreover, the lay panel member serves for a continuing term instead of a single case. Most other common law countries employ juries only in exceptional types of civil litigation, such as defamation cases. In contrast, in the United States trial by jury is constitutionally guaranteed in criminal cases and in most civil cases involving a substantial amount in controversy. Jury trial in civil cases, as well as being constitutionally guaranteed, is regularly employed and enjoys strong popularity. Far from being a constitutional relic, jury trial is the usual form of trial and is the model for trials in which a jury is not employed.

As explained in chapter 2, the federal government and the state governments each have independent court systems. All except Louisiana have a constitutional guaranty of jury trial. The guaranty in the federal court system is provided in the Seventh Amendment to the Constitution, a part of the Bill of Rights adopted in 1791. It provides: "In Suits at common law, where the value in controversy shall exceed twenty dollars, the right of trial by jury shall be preserved, and no fact tried by a jury, shall be otherwise re-examined in any Court of the United States, thus according to the rules of the common law." The counterpart language in the constitutions of the states is substantially similar.

Broadly speaking, the guaranty applies in all cases in which the remedy sought is money damages. This relationship between jury trial and damages actions derives from the facts, first, that jury trial is guaranteed in actions "at law"—meaning those that historically were within the competence of the common law courts—and, second, that the remedy afforded in common law courts ordinarily is that of damages. In cases within the jury trial guaranty, either party may demand jury trial; only if both parties waive the right is the case assigned for trial to a judge without a jury.

The guaranty of jury trial has been liberally interpreted in the modern era. Between 1870 and 1940 many judges, lawyers, and legal scholars disparaged the jury system as being inconsistent with rational legal science; in that intellectual climate, interpretation of the jury trial guaranty was unsympathetic. However, the jury system has enjoyed strong reaffirmation in the last half-century. Particularly influential in safeguarding and expanding the right of jury trial was Justice Hugo Black of the U.S. Supreme Court. Justice Black, who served on the Court from 1937 to 1972, was a strongly committed "populist," reflecting his experience as a lawyer in Alabama and later a senator from that state. As he asserted in a leading decision confirming a broad scope for jury trial, "only under the most imperative circumstances" can the right to jury trial be denied.[1]

"Suits at common law" are to be distinguished from suits in equity and proceedings in admiralty, probate, and divorce. Historically, suits in the latter categories were adjudicated by a judge without a jury. Accordingly, the jury trial guaranty does not apply in these types of civil litigation. Strictly speaking, a suit at common law is one in which the right and remedy were afforded by the common law writ system. As explained in chapter 1, this system enforced various specific legal wrongs, such as trespass and breach of contract. If limited to such cases, the constitutional right of jury trial would be narrowly confined to actions framed under specific common law writs. However, under modern interpretation of the constitutional provision, the right is broadly available in actions for damages, whether the right being enforced derives from old common law or from modern extensions of the common law, such as the law governing misrepresentation in commercial cases. It is also available in actions based on statutory rights providing a damages remedy or civil penalties.[2] The right does not apply when the remedy sought is an injunction, for such a proceeding is still considered to be one in equity.

Composition and Selection of the Jury

Traditionally, the jury consisted of citizens registered to vote, a requirement which for many years excluded women and members of racial minorities. Today, all persons of voting age are potential jurors. Traditionally, the jury consisted of twelve members. However, federal courts now use a six-person jury, as do many states. Traditionally, the verdict was required to be unanimous, but many states provide that a verdict requires only five votes out of six or nine out of twelve. The unanimity requirement has been relaxed to reduce the risk of a "hung jury"—one that cannot come to agreement; if the jury cannot reach the required vote among themselves, there is no verdict and a mistrial results, requiring another trial.

All eligible persons residing in the court's venue are enrolled on a jury service list. Under modern law, this list is constituted from the voter list, the list of licensed vehicle drivers, and other public lists which in combination are broadly inclusive of the adult population. From the jury service list are drawn the names of enough persons to fill jury panels for immediately scheduled cases. The persons so selected report to the court building and constitute the jury pool. From the jury pool, prospective jurors are assigned to each trial courtroom. These procedures are now done by computer.

In the courtroom, the judge trying a specific case presides over selection of the persons who will finally constitute the jury in that case. The selection procedure varies from state to state and to some extent from judge to judge. However, it usually is as follows: The judge initially addresses the prospective jurors, identifying the parties, the transaction involved in the case, and the advocates. The judge then inquires whether any prospective juror has prior acquaintance with the people or the event involved. Those having such acquaintance are excused. Prospective jurors will have completed questionnaires asking their name, age, sex, address, occupation, and prior experience in litigation. This personal information is the basis of specific questions to each juror about background that could prejudice a juror's disposition toward the case. This questioning is called the *voir dire* examination, from the Old French term for "say the truth." In federal courts and some state courts, the judge conducts voir dire. In most state courts the advocates do so, which permits them to probe jury personalities and attitudes.

A prospective juror's response to voir dire questioning that indicates relationship to the parties, or other source of possible prejudice, is a basis for disqualification through a "challenge for cause." Jurors who pass this challenge are provisionally selected. Each side also has a limited number of peremptory challenges—for example, three in federal civil cases. A peremptory challenge requires no justification except that it may not be used to exclude jurors on the basis of race; it is a means by which a party can exclude a juror whose attitude appears threatening or unreliable. The trial jury consists of those who survive challenge for cause and peremptory challenge. They are then sworn to their duty and officially seated.

Voir dire examination and exercise of peremptory challenges are important procedural rights. They protect against jurors who have ties of friendship or common interest with one of the parties. Jury selection is also a subtle game. Each side seeks to seat attractive jurors, to exclude unsympathetic jurors, and to neutralize the opposing party's efforts in the reverse direction. Many experienced trial lawyers consider it the most important aspect of trying a jury case. When the game of jury selection is over, the trial is ready to begin.

Admissibility of Evidence

All procedural systems have rules governing legal proof. Some of these rules address admissibility of evidence—determining whether certain types of evidence may properly be received, such as testimony from the parties themselves. Other rules address the sufficiency of the evidence—determining whether the evidence establishes the facts necessary for a judgment in the case. The American rules, although similar in many respects to those in other countries, are primarily responsive to proof problems in jury trial, while the rules elsewhere are responsive to proof problems in cases decided by judges.

The fact that American evidence rules are designed for jury trial leads to one important concept found in other legal systems but generally absent in American law. The concept is that of the weight or force of particular types of proof. For example, it was a classic evidentiary rule of some of the civil law systems that the court was bound by a party's statement that was against that party's interest: the court was obliged to determine the facts in accordance with the party's statement against interest. The corresponding common law rule is that such a statement, called "an admission against interest," is admissible but can be discounted if the jury is more impressed by other evidence. The distinction between a binding rule concerning the weight of evidence, and merely treating such evidence as part of the proof considered as a whole, probably has limited practical significance. However, as a conceptual problem the idea of binding rules of evidence has occupied a large place in civil law jurisprudence.

In American procedure the rules governing admissibility of evidence are called the law of evidence. Generally, the same rules of admissibility apply in civil and criminal cases alike, but the law of criminal evidence has more restrictions favoring the accused. Generally, the same rules of admissibility apply in cases tried before a judge as in those tried before a jury, but they are administered with greater flexibility.

The law of evidence is primarily administered by the trial judge, who responds to endeavors by one party to present an item of evidence and by the other to block its admission. Secondarily, the law of evidence is administered by the appellate court, which determines whether the trial judge's rulings in admitting and excluding evidence were erroneous, and if so, whether serious unfairness resulted. Finally, the law of evidence provides guidelines for the advocates concerning presentations of the evidence. The law of evidence is thus a discourse among judges and lawyers about the proof that may be presented to juries.

The rules of evidence deal with problems in four general categories: relevance; competence; privilege; and prejudicial and cumulative evidence.

The rule concerning the relevance of evidence is superficially simple: relevant evidence is admissible and irrelevant evidence is not. However, complex epistemological problems lurk beneath this dichotomy. First, there is often doubt about precisely what issues are in dispute and whether a specific item of evidence tends to prove or disprove the issue. For example, in a motor vehicle case, does the allegation that the driver was not careful include the issue of whether the vehicle's brakes were working properly? If the issue of defective brakes is implicated by an allegation that the driver was not careful, then evidence that the brakes were defective is relevant; if that issue is held not to be implicated, the evidence is irrelevant. Further than this, if the issue is not implicated, the evidence is prejudicial, for it invites the jury to consider faults on the part of the driver that are extraneous to the issues properly before the court.

More deeply, not everyone thinks the same way about proof. Proof of facts in litigation, like arriving at factual conclusions in ordinary life, is a complicated mental process. It involves a combination of logical, associative, and analogical reasoning whose pathways are affected by individual experience and therefore differ somewhat from one person to another. It is common knowledge, for example, that young people think differently from older adults about what constitutes a safe speed to drive, and that there are divergent folklore theories about how to determine when another person is telling the truth.

Hence, the rule requiring that evidence be relevant is to some extent arbitrary in its application. Judges differ among themselves over close questions of relevance, and over the admissibility of specific evidence in specific circumstances. However, the experience of judges in administering justice yields a generally shared viewpoint concerning relevance. The advocates adapt their efforts to prove a case accordingly.

The rules governing competence and privilege reflect more general policies, some of them forensic and some based on other social considerations. These rules exclude evidence that would be relevant and probative.

Salient among the problems of competence are those concerning disqualification of parties as witnesses and the hearsay rule. In many civil law systems, as observed in chapter 4, parties are not permitted to testify. The premise is that the interest of parties would induce them to distort their testimony or to lie. The parties can be personally examined by the judge in civil law systems, but such an examination theoretically is intended to clarify the legal and factual issues in the case and to try to reach a settlement. The rule excluding party testimony seems strange to an American observer. Perhaps the explanation for the civil law rule is that it prevents testimonial conflicts that might be embarrassing to the parties' social standing, and shields the judge from having to decide cases on the basis of party credibility. The American rule is that interest in the outcome of the litigation is not a ground for excluding testimony, but it is a factor that may be elicited through cross-examination and used in argument criticizing the testimony.

Another important rule is that which excludes hearsay evidence. Hearsay is a second-hand report of the matter in question, rather than a statement based on direct observation. Thus, "I saw the car hit the pedestrian" is a statement of an observation and is admissible, while the statement "The policeman said the car hit the pedestrian" is hearsay concerning whether the car actually hit the pedestrian, and is inadmissible. The latter statement ordinarily would be excluded under American procedure on the premise that juries may too readily give credit to hearsay. In the other legal systems, the statement would be admissible in civil cases but would be regarded cautiously.

Strict application of the hearsay rule imposes serious obstacles to relevant proof in cases involving voluminous documents. As noted below, documents are admissible only if authenticated, and authentication usually requires testimony of a witness about the circumstances in which the document originated. Supplying such authentication is usually easy where a few documents are involved, such as the principal contract in a simple sale transaction. However, commercial litigation can involve hundreds of documents. In such cases, a witness rarely will be available to testify that every document in a file is regular and genuine; the most that can be said is that, to the best of the witness's knowledge, the documents in the file had originated in the ordinary course of business. Under modern evidence law, this is now sufficient authentication of business and government records.

Another category of exclusionary rules includes those of privilege. The American privilege rules are discussed in chapter 6, because in modern civil litigation questions of privilege usually arise at the stage of pretrial discovery. However, the privilege rules evolved historically in the context of trial evidence, and they still apply at trial. The privileges most frequently involved in civil trials are those covering attorney-client and physician-patient communications. The privilege excludes only the communications as such, for example, the discussion between attorney and client concerning those facts; it does not preclude inquiring into the witness's knowledge of the facts about which the communications were made. Thus it is permissible to ask the witness, "Did you see the car before it hit you?" It is impermissible to ask, "Did you tell your attorney whether you saw the car before it hit you?"

The rules of privilege exclude relevant evidence that would help resolve contested issues. Evidentiary privileges rest on the premise that preserving in general the confidentiality of such communications has greater social value than improving the accuracy of fact-finding in specific legal disputes. The rules concerning privilege in other legal systems generally correspond to those in the U.S., indicating the important human considerations underlying them. The civil law accordingly prohibits inquiry into communications between doctor and patient, advocate and client, and husband and wife.

Finally, the evidentiary rules exclude prejudicial and cumulative testimony. These rules safeguard fair and orderly procedure but are necessarily imprecise in their application, which is largely in the discretion of the trial judge. "Prejudicial" evidence is proof that has some probative value but also invites illegitimate inferences. For example, it is ordinarily impermissible to prove, in a motor vehicle accident civil case, that the driver was charged by the police with a penal violation in the incident. The fact that the police concluded that the driver was at fault tends to prove that he actually was at fault. However, the evidence also is prejudicial because it invites the conclusion that the driver must have been at fault if the police charged him so. Another form of prejudicial evidence is proof showing a party's wealth, which also is ordinarily excluded. "Cumulative" evidence is proof that has probative value and is not inadmissible under the exclusionary rules, but adds little to proof already received. For example, if three independent witnesses have testified consistently to a fact in issue, the court may refuse testimony from a fourth witness.

The four categories of rules—the requirement of relevance, the exclusionary rule concerning competence, the rules of privilege, and the discretionary rules concerning prejudicial and cumulative evidence—regulate the jury's decision of factual issues and its application of the proper legal standards to the facts. This form of control complements that exercised through the judge's supervision of the trial, the judge's instructions to the jury, and rules governing secrecy and propriety in the jury's deliberations. However, these rules are merely external controls on the jury's decision process. There is no procedure for examining how the jury actually arrives at its verdict, except in cases of extreme misbehavior such as juror drunkenness during trial or a juror's communication with outside sources about the case. The jury decision process is protected as a "black box"; the rules of evidence determine only what goes into the box.

Sequence of Presentation

The basic rule in trial presentation is that the plaintiff first presents its case, then the defendant counters with its case. Within this framework, each party presents its witnesses one after another. The party presenting a witness does so through direct examination, whereupon the opposing parties may cross-examine that witness. To facilitate the jury's comprehension of the case as a whole, the advocates make introductory statements before the evidence is presented and concluding arguments after all the evidence has been received.

At the beginning of trial, after seating the jury, the judge usually provides an orientation to the case. The judge introduces the parties and their counsel, describes the general subject of the case, and outlines the duties of the jury, the judge, and counsel. The jury is told that its function will be to decide the facts under instructions concerning the law provided by the judge; that the advocates' statements are not law or evidence but only means of presenting the evidence; that the jurors should reserve their conclusions until all the evidence is received and there is opportunity to discuss it among themselves; that they should not discuss the case with others or among themselves until their deliberations; and that they should be fair-minded toward all parties. Jurors usually take these responsibilities very seriously.

After the judge completes this introduction, the advocate for the plaintiff makes an opening statement, which is a narrative of the evidence to be offered in plaintiff's case. Experienced advocates give detailed, factual narratives and do not go beyond what they can prove because they want the jury to trust them and to believe their evidence. In their opening presentation, they also seek in a controlled way to excite interest, attention, and emotional engagement. Openly inflammatory argument is not permitted.

After the opening statement on behalf of plaintiff, the defendant may make a responsive opening statement. However, defendant has the option of deferring its statement until beginning the presentation of its case, which follows after plaintiff's case has been presented.

Following the opening statement for plaintiff, the advocate for plaintiff calls the witnesses. The order in which witnesses are presented is fashioned by the advocate taking into account the logical sequence of the evidence, dramatic effect, and witnesses' other schedule commitments. The plaintiff himself or herself almost always is presented, either as the first or last witness.

A witness's testimony is elicited by the advocate's questions, called direct examination. Parts of a typical sequence could be as follows:

Q: Please state your name for the court and jury.
A: _____.
Q: Please give us your home address and where you work.
A: _____.
Q: What is your occupation?
A: _____.
. . .
Q: Were you struck by a car on July 31, 1992?
A: _____.
Q: Where did this incident occur?
A: _____.
Q: Were you on foot at the time?
A: _____.
Q: At what location in relation to the street were you when you were hit?

A: _____.

Q: Did you suffer any loss of physical function following the accident?

. . .

Q: Do you still suffer loss of motion in your right leg?

A: _____.

Q: Can you tell the jury what limitations you have in using that leg?

A: _____.

. . .

After completing the questioning, the advocate says, "No further questions" or, "Pass the witness." Cross-examination then ensues.

The common law procedure of direct examination stands in sharp contrast to the traditional civil law procedure. Under the civil law, a party must indicate before trial the witnesses that it wishes the court to examine and must supply a detailed written summary of the testimony expected from each witness. A copy of the summary must be given to the other side, which may specify supplemental questions that it wishes the judge to ask. At trial, the judge examines the witnesses by following the summaries provided by the parties. The judge goes beyond the summary only if necessary to clarify the witness's testimony, and ordinarily will not extend the questioning to other matters. The advocates for the parties may interject requests to the judge for clarifying questions, but it is within the judge's discretion whether to pursue them. The court's record of the testimony is a summary dictated by the judge to the court clerk when the witness's examination has been completed. This summary will be even more synoptic and formal than the summary from which the testimony originated.

In contrast, the direct examination in the common law system is conducted by the advocate, through step-by-step questions that elicit more or less extemporaneous answers. The opposing party will not know precisely the testimony to be forthcoming from the witness, although the discovery deposition of the witness is usually a good forecast. If there is significant discrepancy between the witness's testimony at trial and that given in deposition, the witness may be cross-examined about the inconsistency. Moreover, under the rules of evidence, when a witness relies on written notes or a written summary, they must be provided to the opposing party as a basis for cross-examination. Furthermore, reliance on such notes may indicate that the witness has little or no independent recollection of the matters about which he or she is testifying. Ordinarily, the testimony of a witness is relatively spontaneous. Testimony that appears to be carefully rehearsed usually will be regarded with suspicion.

The witness's direct testimony is the background for cross-examination. In form, cross-examination is essentially similar to direct examination, except that "leading" questions are more freely permitted. Leading questions are ones suggesting the answer. However, since cross-examination is conducted by the opposing advocate, it is often correspondingly searching and aggressive. The advocate will have carefully indexed the witness's deposition testimony, which may comprise several volumes of transcript. The advocate will also have kept careful notes as the witness was testifying in direct examination. The advocate is not required to reveal in advance the questions that will be asked on cross-examination. The interrogation is often a game of cat and mouse.

Parts of a typical cross-examination could be:

Q: You didn't actually see the car before the incident, did you?

A: _____.

Q: Well, if you saw the car for only an instant, you couldn't fix what rate of speed it was traveling, could you?

. . .

Q: Now your leg doesn't keep you from going to work, does it?

A: _____.

. . .

Upon completion of cross-examination, the advocate who originally questioned the witness is allowed further questions addressed
to matters raised in the cross-examination. This is called redirect
examination and is usually very brief.

Each examination is monitored by the opposing advocate, who
objects to questions that are irrelevant, misleading, harassing, or
otherwise improper. The judge rules on objections. A typical sequence could be as follows:

> *Defense lawyer continuing cross-examination:*
> Now you couldn't really see the car at all, could you?
> *Plaintiff's lawyer:*
> Objection, Your Honor: repetitive. The question has been
> asked and answered.
> *Judge:*
> Sustained.

Alternately, the judge may overrule the objection on the grounds
that such repetition is permissible in cross-examination.

Sequences of questioning in a trial conducted by experienced
advocates usually have relatively few interruptions. Experienced
advocates know how to ask unobjectionable questions and know
also that objections are counterproductive unless really necessary.
However, where crucial evidence is involved and arguably should
be excluded, the interchanges between the advocates can be intense
and persistent: intense because much turns on whether the evidence
is allowed, and persistent because the proponent may try several
approaches to eliciting the vital testimony. The situation can get
out of hand if the judge is not attentive and firm.

Documentary evidence requires supporting testimony for its authentication, unless authenticity is conceded. Authentication consists of testimony by a witness who identifies the document and
affirms its genuineness. A typical exchange could be as follows:

> Q: And you are the records clerk at Mercy Hospital?
> A: Yes.

Q: I hand you Plaintiff's Exhibit 6 for identification. Please tell us what that is.

A: This is a correct full copy of the hospital record for John Smith, the plaintiff in this case, for the period July 31 to August 5, 1991.

Q: Your Honor, I move admission of Exhibit 6.

Judge: Unless there is objection, it will be received.

Because the authentication procedure usually is merely technical, the parties customarily stipulate the admissibility of all documents whose authenticity is undisputed. In cases involving many documents, disputed issues of authentication will be resolved in pretrial rulings.

When plaintiff's evidence is completed, that evidence as a whole constitutes plaintiff's "case in chief." Plaintiff then "rests."

At this point, defendant may challenge the legal validity of the plaintiff's case. For example, defendant may contend that an essential element has not been proved, or that the evidence clearly discloses that there is no liability on defendant's part. These contentions are logically similar to the motion to dismiss for failure to state a claim, discussed in chapter 6. However, at trial the target of this objection is the plaintiff's evidence, whereas at pretrial the target is the plaintiff's pleading. If the judge sustains the challenge to the sufficiency of the plaintiff's evidence, judgment for defendant is directed. The jury therefore will have no function and will be discharged. If the judge overrules the challenge, or if no challenge is made, defendant then presents its evidence.

Defendant's presentation is called its case in chief. The procedure employed is the same as in plaintiff's case. That is, defendant's witnesses are presented in sequence, determined by defense counsel. Each witness is examined first by the advocate presenting the witness, then cross-examined by plaintiff's advocate. Upon finishing presentation of its case, defendant rests. Plaintiff may challenge the sufficiency of defendant's evidence regarding any affirmative defense according to the same logic as plaintiff's evidence might be challenged by defendant. However, if both sides have presented a minimum of evidence supporting their respective positions, there are factual issues to be resolved by the jury. Accordingly, when the evidence is in conflict, the trial must continue.

If matters have come up in defendant's case that plaintiff should be allowed to rebut, plaintiff introduces rebuttal evidence. Such evidence usually is brief.

When all the evidence is in, the advocates address the jury with final arguments. Plaintiff's advocate makes the opening argument, defendant responds, and plaintiff then closes. The judge fixes the time limits for those arguments, usually an hour or several hours per side, depending on the complexity of the case. Latitude is allowed for emotional appeal in the advocate's closing arguments, but an experienced advocate also seeks to suggest that the evidence for his or her side has overwhelming logical force.

After the advocates' arguments, the judge instructs the jury. The judge's instructions are statements of the governing legal principles, presented in as simplified terms as possible. For example, the instruction concerning the standard of conduct in an accident case would be similar to the following:

Judge: I instruct you that "negligence" consists of failure to use that care which a person of ordinary prudence would reasonably use in the circumstances. It does not consist of slight failure in this respect, nor is gross fault required. The standard is that of ordinary reasonable care.

There is a formulaic quality to jury instructions. While they must be as clear as possible, they also must be technically accurate, for their accuracy may be scrutinized in appellate review. Standardized instructions are used in recurring types of cases. Juries usually seem to get the general idea from the judge's instructions, even if they do not understand all the legal subtleties.

Upon completion of the instructions, the jury retires to a closed meeting room for deliberation. They elect a foreman, who presides, and then discuss the case and vote upon a verdict. When sufficient votes establish a winner, the foreman signs the proper verdict form, in favor of plaintiff or defendant as the case may be. The jury then returns to court and, in the presence of the advocates, the foreman reports the verdict. The judge asks each juror to verify that their verdict is as reported. The jury is then discharged.

Sufficiency of Evidence

A fundamental concept in jury trial is that of the sufficiency of the evidence, which concerns the probative weight of evidence necessary to submit the case to the jury. The rule is as follows: Plaintiff must present evidence from which the jury could reasonably find a verdict for plaintiff; otherwise the judge dismisses the case for failure of proof. The same principle applies to defendant with respect to affirmative defenses and counterclaims, as to which defendant has the burden of proof. If the sufficiency standard is fulfilled, the jury decides what to believe from the conflicting evidence.

The purpose of the rule concerning sufficiency of the evidence is to preclude the jury from rendering a verdict for which there is no substantial supporting evidence. A jury might do so, for example, because it is biased toward a party or because it wishes to apply a different legal standard from that in the judge's instructions. However, the judge determines whether the evidence is such that a jury could rationally arrive at a verdict on the basis of that evidence. Accordingly, it is said that the sufficiency of the evidence is a question of law.

More precisely, the rule concerning sufficiency of the evidence empowers the judge to determine the range of factual possibility that the evidence rationally encompasses. Although the jury has a wide scope in applying law to fact, and within that scope it cannot be overruled by the judge, the sufficiency of the evidence standard imposes boundaries on the jury's discretion. This concept gives effect to the rule of law, for it limits the jury's power to disregard the law. The concept also requires maintaining a systematic distinction between issues of law, which are for the judge, and issues of fact, which are within the limits of the sufficiency standard for the jury.

There is no direct counterpart to this concept in the civil law system. Since the first-instance judge in the civil law system decides questions of fact as well as of law, the judge does not need to ask him- or herself whether the evidence would reasonably support a conclusion by someone else, that is, the jury. Rather, the judge directly proceeds to an independent conclusion concerning the evidence. Reaching this conclusion requires the judge to ask whether the evidence provided by the party with the burden of proof persuades him or her to decide in that party's favor. In a case in which the judge decides the facts, the questions of sufficiency of evidence and the persuasive effect of evidence thus merge into a single question: "What does the judge conclude from the evidence?" In practice, this is also the situation in cases tried without a jury in American procedure.

Verdict, Judgment, and Posttrial Motions

The jury's verdict is a finding, not a judgment. The distinction is between a conclusion as to what the outcome should be, which is the verdict, and the court's official act adjudicating the controversy, which is the judgment. The verdict speaks in terms of "We, the jury, find. . . ." The judgment speaks in terms of "Judgment is hereby entered. . . ." The jury's verdict is either a money award in favor of the plaintiff or a verdict for defendant that plaintiff "take nothing"; it is the court's function to enter judgment accordingly. The judgment constitutes a basis for enforcement procedures if the losing party does not voluntarily comply with the judgment. The judgment is also the predicate for appeal.

However, before taking an appeal, a party dissatisfied with the verdict may request the trial court for corrective action. Indeed, requesting such relief is often required before pursuing an appeal. Corrective action may address procedural errors in the trial or insufficiency of evidence to support the verdict. Request for corrective action is made by a motion for new trial or by a motion for judgment notwithstanding the verdict.

A motion for new trial, as its name implies, asks the court to order the case to be retried. This is an appropriate remedy when serious procedural error occurred at trial, for example: serious misbehavior of a party or an advocate, such as creating disorder or making flagrantly unfair statements; misbehavior of a juror, such as using personal knowledge of the facts; misbehavior of the judge, such as intemperate remarks; outside interference, such as an attempt by an outsider to influence the jury. If a motion for new trial is granted, the case will be tried anew, without, it is hoped, repetition of the contaminating incident. Only serious disturbances justify a new trial, and their occurrence in civil cases is infrequent.

A new trial may also be granted when the judge concludes that the verdict was against the weight of the evidence. Exercise of this power depends on a subtle distinction. The distinction is between evidence that meets the standard of legal sufficiency described above and evidence that, although sufficient, should not have convinced the jury. This distinction in weightiness of evidence is intuitively coherent, even though its verbalization is abstruse. In effect, the concept permits the judge to reevaluate the correctness of the jury's verdict and on that basis to require submission of the case to another jury through a new trial. However, it does not allow the judge to enter judgment directly. If the jury in the second trial reaches the same result, that verdict will ordinarily be accepted as the basis for judgment. The judge's power to set aside a verdict that he considers unwarranted may also be exercised where the judge concludes that the jury's assessment of damages was inadequate or excessive.

A judge may enter judgment notwithstanding the verdict where, looking back at the proof, the judge concludes that the evidence is legally insufficient to support the verdict. The question immediately presents itself: If the judge has concluded after verdict that the evidence was legally insufficient, why did the judge not act on that conclusion before the verdict and direct judgment at that time? Through the procedure called a directed verdict, the judge is empowered to direct judgment before verdict where the judge concludes that the evidence is legally insufficient. (See preceding section.) Why was this not done?

There are two explanations for such a delayed preemption of the jury's authority to decide the facts. First, the judge may simply have changed his or her mind after reflecting more fully on the evidence. What initially seemed sufficient evidence may appear in retrospect not to have been so.

The second possible explanation is more complicated. The judge is conscious that the question of whether the evidence is legally insufficient is a matter concerning which the appellate court may disagree. With this in mind, at the close of the evidence and before submitting the case to the jury, the judge can approach the problem of the sufficiency of the evidence in the following way: If I grant a directed verdict, so that the jury makes no decision, my decision in that respect may be reversed on appeal; in that event, the case will have to be retried to a new jury; however, if I refuse to grant a directed verdict, the jury will make a decision; if the jury finds as I believe the evidence clearly requires, then the verdict will be proper and I will have made no ruling that the appellate court might reverse; on the other hand, if the jury comes to a verdict that I believe is against the evidence, I can then enter a judgment notwithstanding the verdict; if the appellate court agrees with me, it will affirm; if the appellate court believes the evidence was sufficient, it can reinstate the verdict and order judgment accordingly; in any event, a new trial will be unnecessary.

The foregoing corrective measures usually are taken only upon motion of a party. In some circumstances the court can act on its own initiative, but this is rarely required because the advocates ordinarily will make the necessary motions.

The judge's review of a verdict is the point of most critical tension in the system of jury trial. The principle of jury trial is that justice should be an expression of ordinary citizens' conceptions of right and wrong. On this basis, the jury's conclusion about the evidence should be conclusive. However, the principle of the rule of law is that justice should not depend on personalities and peculiar circumstances. Sometimes, ordinary citizens' conceptions of right and wrong, expressed in a verdict, depend upon personalities and peculiar circumstances. On this basis, the jury's view of right and wrong can conflict with that expressed in the law. This is an inherent and unavoidable tension. The jury system makes ordinary citizens an integral part of the administration of the law, but it also invites them to criticize and in extreme cases to disregard the law.

The same tension in doing justice—between general legal principles and peculiar specific circumstances—of course exists in other legal systems. In the civil law system, the corresponding tension occurs in the second-instance court's review of the first-instance court's decision; an appeal in the civil law system often is functionally equivalent to a motion for new trial in the jury trial system. Both systems use terminology that obfuscates the issues of epistemology and legal authority that are involved. Underlying the obscure terminology is irreducible conflict over different understandings of justice—justice according to general rules of law and justice according to human interest in a specific case.

Trial before a Judge without a Jury

Many cases in the American system are tried by the court without a jury. Such a trial is conducted before a single judge, who decides both the factual and legal issues. The judge's determination is expressed in findings of fact and conclusions of law, followed by judgment. In general, a judge's findings of fact are accorded the same weight by an appellate court as the verdict of a jury.

Cases are tried without a jury when the proceeding is in equity—for example, a suit for an injunction. So also in an action to enforce a statutory right in which jury trial has been precluded—for example, suits for compensatory damages against the government. So also when both parties waive jury, which is often done in commercial and financial litigation and in cases where a jury is unlikely to be sympathetic to the human element.

A trial before a judge follows the structure of a jury trial, with pretrial discovery being completed before trial. However, greater flexibility of scheduling is possible, because the jury's convenience need not be considered. Accordingly, key issues may be pursued through separate discovery and trial before remaining issues are considered. Within the trial, the same sequence as in a jury trial is usually followed: plaintiff's case in chief, then defendant's case, then rebuttal. However, opening statements and closing arguments are usually shorter or may be presented in writing rather than orally.

Examination of witnesses proceeds as in a jury trial, with questioning of each witness by the proponent advocate and cross-examination by the opponent, through the array of witnesses. Initial orientation questions usually will be fewer, and answers will be given in longer narratives. The judge will freely interject his or her own questions and expedite attention to key issues.

When all evidence is received, the judge may ask the parties for written briefs addressed to the facts and to the law. Often the judge reserves decision until he or she has reviewed the verbatim transcript of the testimony. When the judge has reached a conclusion, he or she may ask the prevailing party to prepare proposed findings of fact and conclusions of law. This saves the judge the labor of drafting these determinations and allows the party to guard against omissions. However, using the party's draft results in a highly formal decision that does not reflect the judge's thought process. The primary objective in employing the document is not to explain the decision but to make a formally correct record. Perhaps it is anomalous that American procedure, so "real" in many respects, is so formal when it comes to the decision of a trial judge in a nonjury case.

CHAPTER EIGHT

Procedural Variations

Litigation that involves more than two parties is governed by rules of "joinder" of parties. Related to these are the rules governing joinder of claims, which facilitate assertion of multiple claims between any two parties and also claims among multiple parties. Although the joinder of parties rules are technically complicated, the organizing concept is that all parties having a claim or liability arising out of a transaction or series of related transactions may be brought into the case. There are certain restrictions, notably those in federal courts springing from limitations on their competence in diversity of citizenship cases. Generally speaking, the initiative to join additional parties is with the original parties, primarily the plaintiff. The court has limited authority to compel joinder of parties.

The rules facilitating party joinder are as follows: permissive joinder of defendants; permissive joinder of plaintiffs; cross-claims and impleader; joinder of necessary parties; intervention; interpleader; and class actions. In addition, a party prosecuted as a defendant may counterclaim against the plaintiff.

Permissive joinder of defendants allows the plaintiff to join as defendants all wrongdoers who acted concertedly or concurrently in the incident causing plaintiff injury. Thus, in a multivehicle highway accident, drivers and owners of all vehicles involved may be made defendants; in a breach of contract suit against several defaulting obligors, all the obligors may be made defendants; in a pollution case, all sources contributing to the pollution may be made defendants. Furthermore, if plaintiff is injured by successive wrongful acts contributing to a single injury, all those involved in the sequence may be defendants. For example, if plaintiff is injured in a vehicle accident, and thereafter suffers medical malpractice in being treated for the injuries, the action may be brought against the vehicle driver and owner, the hospital, and the doctors participating in treatment.

Ordinarily, the plaintiff will avail itself of the permissive joinder rule to join all those potentially liable for his damage. Doing so permits plaintiff to employ a single discovery procedure for developing the evidence and to present all his contentions in one trial. This strategy also has the advantage that the various defendants may try to blame each other, thus strengthening plaintiff's case. Correlatively, plaintiff avoids the risk that each defendant, if sued separately, will blame someone else involved, a tactic by which all defendants could eventually escape liability.

Permissive joinder of plaintiffs allows all persons injured in a single incident to assert their claims in a single action. For example, several members of a family injured in a vehicle accident may join in suit against the alleged wrongdoers. So also victims of a common fraudulent scheme. The advantages of joining as plaintiffs are similar to those in joinder of defendants: unified discovery and a unified trial. There can be disadvantages, however, especially if one of the claimants may be partly at fault concerning the injury. For example, when one of the family members injured in a vehicle accident was driver of the car in which they were riding, a jury might attribute the driver's negligence to other family members, even though legally no such attribution is authorized. So also, if victims of a common fraudulent scheme include sophisticated business people as well as unsophisticated householders, it may be strategically unwise for them to join in one action, because the effect of contributory fault will differ among them.

Other practical considerations influence joinder decisions. For example, a plaintiff may refrain from joining someone against whom a valid claim could be made but who, if spared from being sued, might give evidence more favorable to plaintiff.

Another influential factor is the situation of the advocates for the parties. When one advocate represents all the claimants, he or she usually will join them all as plaintiffs in a single action. When different advocates represent various claimants, they are likely to bring separate actions. These decisions are based on practical considerations. Cooperation may be inhibited by the advocates' strategies and forensic styles, and also by effects on the advocates' fees. If claimants with different advocates join in one action, then one advocate ordinarily must take a lead role in dealing with the court and with the opposing parties, a role that may entitle the advocate to a greater share of the fees due from the claimants as a group. Unless these matters can be negotiated, a cooperative single action may be impossible.

These considerations underscore that decisions concerning joinder are made primarily by the parties rather than by the court, and that in practice they usually are made by the advocates and are influenced by their interests. However, the court is empowered to supersede the parties' joinder decisions to an important extent. This is done by consolidation or severance.

The court may consolidate actions concerning the same incident that have been brought separately; a suit that appears too complicated may be severed into separate actions. In practice, a single coordinated discovery phase usually is held for all suits involving the same incident. The trial stage may be structured according to the similarity of issues as they affect various plaintiffs and defendants. The court has broad discretion in exercising these powers.

Operating concurrently with the joinder of parties rules are the joinder of claims rules. At common law distinct claims could not be asserted if they required different forms of action. This restriction was abolished in the Federal Rules of Civil Procedure. In modern procedure a plaintiff may assert any claim against any defendant arising out of the common incident.

Augmenting the permissive joinder of party rules are several auxiliary procedures. One of these is that of cross-claim, whereby a claim may be asserted by one coparty against another. For example, when two defendants are sued, they may cross-claim for allocation between them of any liability imposed on both of them in favor of the plaintiff. A similar procedure is impleader. Under this procedure, a defendant may bring in as a subordinate defendant anyone (not already joined) who may be liable for indemnifying the defendant against the liability asserted in the principal claim against defendant.

Another auxiliary is the necessary party rule. This rule requires the joinder of persons whose interests could jeopardize the coherence of the adjudication between those who are already parties to the action. Thus, joint obligors in a contract ordinarily must be made parties defendant so that their legal responsibilities to each other may be resolved. A related rule is that governing intervention. A person not originally made a party may petition to become a party where his or her interests are interdependent with those of the original parties.

The court has broad discretion in administering the necessary party and intervention rules. Two objectives, sometimes conflicting, must be accommodated by these rules. On one hand, it is desirable that all related claims be resolved in one proceeding, thus furthering consistency and efficiency in adjudication. On the other hand, the litigation should not be made too complicated. Also, weight is given to the original plaintiff's preference concerning the scope of the litigation. Plaintiff has the burden of initiative in the action, and ultimately the burden of proof; these burdens can be heavier if the litigation is enlarged beyond the limits preferred by the plaintiff.

Another joinder rule, called interpleader, is available for controversies involving conflicting claims to a specific fund or specific property. The person holding the fund may bring an action against the various claimants to the fund, requiring that the claims be resolved so that proper distribution can be made. The procedure protects the stakeholder from the risk that separate actions by the claimants could produce inconsistent results, perhaps leaving the stakeholder obligated to more than one of the claimants.

These joinder rules ordinarily permit all claimants and all obligors to become parties to a single litigation, even when the underlying transaction is very complicated. Highly complicated cases often find their way into the federal courts, usually because some of the claims are based on federal law. When diversity jurisdiction is the basis of the federal court's competence, there may be constraints on the court's authority to adjudicate the entire controversy. In diversity actions there must be complete diversity of citizenship between all plaintiffs and all defendants, a requirement that often cannot be fulfilled in complex cases. When this is so, the federal court may either dismiss the action and relegate the case to a state court, or adjudicate the parts of the litigation that it can retain consistent with the complete diversity requirement.

While the complete diversity requirement thus restricts the scope of complex litigation in federal court, the federal courts also have a special authority that is often useful in such cases. In the federal court system, the pretrial phase of separate but related cases can be transferred to one district for unified discovery procedures. Especially when pretrial discovery will be long and complex, pretrial administration in one district promotes consistency and efficiency. Similar efficiencies can be achieved through unofficial cooperative arrangements between state courts of different states and between federal and state courts.

There is strong judicial preference for unified administration of cases in which one incident or transaction results in litigation involving many claimants or defendants. However, the advocates often resist such unification, fearing confusion, delay, and loss of control. These fears are often warranted. Nevertheless, the burden placed on the courts by separate proceedings justifies strong judicial supervision in most complex cases, particularly in the pretrial phase. This is now the accepted procedural policy.

Complex Litigation

The American legal system is now accustomed to litigation of extraordinary complexity. For example, in a case resulting from the financial failure of a business corporation whose stock is traded on a public stock exchange, the claims involved could be as follows:

claims by unpaid creditors of the corporation, asserting that corporate assets were improperly diverted from payment of obligations due them;

claims by stockholders of the corporation, asserting that the corporation's management mishandled its affairs, resulting in loss of their investment;

claims by employees of the corporation, asserting that their pension rights were impaired by the corporation's failure to make required payments into the pension fund;

claims against the corporation's banks, investment advisers, accountants, and lawyers for their fault in causing the losses;

cross-claims among the corporate directors and officers, the banks and investment advisers, and the accountants, auditors, and lawyers for allocation of responsibility among these defendants;

impleader claims against insurance companies that insured the various defendants concerning the scope and extent of the insurance coverage for the losses.

The claims in such a case may well include ones based on federal statutes and regulations, state statutes, and common law. The number of individuals to be examined through discovery in such a case could be twenty or even fifty, in depositions each lasting two or more days and involving five or six lawyers. Hundreds or thousands of documents could be examined and reviewed with witnesses during depositions. Expert witnesses in corporate management, finance accounting, and law will provide analyses and opinions and be subjected to discovery depositions. Charts and financial accounts will be prepared to depict and explain the transactions. In preparation for trial, advocates for each party will spend hours preparing their witnesses for examination and cross-examination at trial.

A major accident—for example, an airplane crash or an oil spill—produces similarly complex litigation. Claims will be made by those suffering death or injury or property loss against those charged with primary or secondary legal responsibility—the companies operating the equipment involved, those that supplied components that may have malfunctioned, governmental agencies that may have been neglectful of their safety responsibilities, and third parties whose acts or omissions may have compounded the loss. Immediately behind the scenes are various liability insurers, which eventually may also become parties to secondary litigation over allocation of the losses.

Such complex litigation is facilitated by the American procedural system: liberal rules concerning joinder of claims and parties; rules allowing investigative discovery through which broad categories of documents can be demanded and intensive deposition interrogation conducted of all possible witnesses; the permissibility of contingent-fee arrangements and the general immunity from liability for an opposing party's attorneys' fees; legislative empowerment of private civil litigation as a regulatory mechanism; liberal rules for measuring damages; and a legal system, supported by public opinion, that has been sympathetic to victims of misfortune.

The proliferation of complex litigation has resulted in repeated calls for reform, but proposals to reduce or simplify complex litigation have typically been superficial. A realistic view recognizes that the uniquely complex forms of American civil litigation are the product of a uniquely complex legal system that is itself the product of a uniquely legalistic culture.

Injunctions

An injunction is a court order directing the defendant to perform a certain act or series of acts, or to refrain from doing so, as distinct from a judgment for damages; the typical jury trial results in a judgment for damages. The typical equity suit, tried without a jury, seeks an injunction.

Injunctions may be awarded in a wide variety of cases, including claims by one private party against another private party. For example, such a remedy could be sought by a landowner suffering from repeated invasions of his or her land by flooding or air pollution or straying animals from an adjacent landowner's property. So also, an injunction might be sought against piracy of business secrets or interference with contract rights. Injunctions may be granted in favor of a government agency against a private party as, for example, against pollution occurring in violation of environmental regulations, or against issuance of securities in violation of the securities laws. Similarly, injunctions may issue in favor of a private party against a government agency or official. For example, a publisher claiming that a government regulation unconstitutionally interferes with freedom of speech may seek an injunction against the official having authority to enforce the regulation. Civil actions for judicial review of administrative action, discussed in chapter 3, often seek an injunctive remedy.

Historically, the remedy of injunction was considered exceptional and required special justification. As noted in chapter 1, a plaintiff seeking an injunction traditionally was required to show that the damages remedy available at law would not adequately remedy the wrong. This requirement, known as the "adequacy test," is still recited in some judicial decisions, but has become nearly obsolete. In modern litigation, an injunction may be awarded when plaintiff shows that violation of its legal interests threatens to be continuing or that damages will not as effectively redress the wrong as requiring defendant to take remedial action.

Injunction cases generally proceed like other litigation tried without a jury. There are pleading and discovery phases, followed by trial. The same rules of evidence and of forensic presentation generally apply. However, there are two important differences between injunction and damages actions, in addition to the fact that juries are not employed in injunction cases. The first difference concerns temporary injunctive relief, which may be granted prior to full hearing of the evidence. The second concerns the scope of judicial discretion in the provisions of the injunction.

Temporary injunctive relief may be obtained where the injury is continuing or where an injury is imminently threatened that could not be fully compensated through an award of damages. Since the case may take weeks or months in the pretrial phase, the plaintiff faces the threat of continuing or irreparable injury. Hence, there may be need for a temporary injunction to prevent or moderate further injury until the merits of the dispute can be fully considered.

Interim relief may consist of a temporary restraining order (TRO), followed by a preliminary injunction. A TRO can be granted upon plaintiff's showing urgent necessity, with very short notice to the defendant or, in extreme cases, no notice at all. However, a hearing must be held as soon as possible to determine whether the temporary protection should continue. An extension, known as a preliminary injunction, can then be granted.

Granting temporary injunctive protection risks injustice because the subsequent plenary trial may determine that plaintiff is not entitled to any relief, or is entitled only to damages. Temporary relief may therefore impose unjust burden and expense on the defendant. On the other hand, if a temporary injunction is not granted, continuing and irreparable damages may result to the plaintiff. These risks are addressed by the trial judge, who tries to ascertain, at the preliminary hearing, how clear and certain is the plaintiff's right and whether temporary protection will impose a serious burden on defendant. This decision involves broad judicial discretion in balancing competing equities.

The judge has similar discretion concerning the terms of final injunctive relief. The court may impose specific and highly restrictive terms, or less onerous ones; it may require that redress be made partly in money damages and partly by corrective action by defendant; it may impose the injunction for an indefinite period or for a limited one; it may require defendant to make reports evidencing compliance; and it may appoint an auxiliary judicial officer to supervise compliance. An injunction may also subsequently be modified to take account of changed conditions. All these variables are committed primarily to the discretion of the trial court judge. They will be modified by an appellate court only if that court is convinced that there was an abuse of discretion.

An especially elaborate form of injunction is the "institutional decree," an injunction requiring, say, a public school, prison, hospital, or business corporation to conform its operations to specified legal requirements. Such decrees have been issued to remedy racial segregation in schools, unsafe and unhealthy conditions in prisons and hospitals, and environmental pollution. Through such a remedy, the court becomes the monitor of the institution during the life of the injunction. When the institution's officials are cooperative, institutional decrees have been very successful in remedying illegal conditions in public institutions. When the officials have not been cooperative, the result is usually continuing legal strife and often frustration of the court's directives.

An injunction takes the form of an order addressed personally to the defendant. For this reason it is sometimes said that an equity decree acts *in personam,* that is, "against the person" of the defendant, as distinct from the matter in which defendant has been engaged. The practical significance of its being such an order is that disobedience may be punished by contempt of court, civil or criminal. Accordingly, as explained in chapter 10, defendant can be fined or jailed in order to enforce compliance.

Class Suits

The class suit is a unique American procedure for handling a large number of similar claims arising out of a single incident. There are two general types of class suits. The first involves claims too small to be economically handled in separate actions. Since the cost of American litigation is high, claims under twenty-five thousand dollars or thereabouts as a practical matter come within this category. The second type of class suit involves an injunction on behalf of many persons subjected to a common wrong, such as racial discrimination committed by an employer against a large group of employees, common injury suffered by corporate stockholders resulting from the company's mismanagement, or injury by an environmental polluter committed against a large group of surrounding residents.

Historically, the class suit developed in equity and was used primarily in cases involving injuries to property rights. The modern class suit developed in the 1960s, aided by amendment of the rules governing class-action procedure and by sympathetic decisions by the courts. The basis for class suits, both historically and in modern times, is the difficulty of adjudicating claims held by members of a large group and the courts' wish to avoid repetitive litigation.

The concept in a class action is that a small number of the injured group volunteer to bring suit on behalf of the whole group. The plaintiffs sue "on behalf of themselves and all other similarly situated," as the complaint will allege. In bringing suit in this representative capacity, the plaintiffs undertake fiduciary duties to the rest of the class, including the duties to treat all claimants alike in measurement and payment of damages; to allocate equitably the cost of litigation among the class members, including the fee for the class's advocate; and, in settling the case, to negotiate terms that are fair to the absentees.

The procedure in a class suit generally follows that in other actions, except for the initial and concluding stages of the litigation. At the initial stage the court must first determine whether the situation justifies a class suit; if that requirement is met, the court must also determine whether the class is adequately represented by the members who have volunteered, and whether the assistance to be provided by their advocate will be sufficient.

The formal requirements of a class suit are as follows: the group of alleged victims must have suffered a common wrong; the group must be so numerous that separate actions by its members are impractical; the claims of the volunteer representatives must be typical of those of the group; and the volunteer representatives must adequately represent the class. If these requirements are met, the action is certified as a class suit and proceeds as such. Otherwise, the class suit aspect is dismissed, leaving the plaintiffs to prosecute their claims as individuals.

As a practical matter, many class suits are organized by the advocates. Most class suits for an injunction are social-action litigation, in which the advocates are paid by activist groups sponsoring the litigation. Most class suits for damages are prosecuted on a contingent fee, where the advocate hopes the judgment or settlement will justify the investment of effort. The court's practical concern at the initial stage of an injunction class suit is whether the common interest of the class is sufficiently defined and whether the supporting group has the resources to carry through. The court's practical concern in contingent-fee class suits for damages is whether the advocate will give priority to the interests of the class rather than to his or her own interests. As a control against exploitation of damage class suits, claimants in such cases have a right to "opt out" of the class: a claimant may exclude him- or herself from the class and proceed with a separate action. In practice, few claimants opt out, because the cost of a separate action is usually prohibitive.

In very unusual circumstances, a class may be a defendant, for example, a suit against corporate stockholders as a group. Essentially the same certification standards must be met as in a plaintiff class.

Special judicial supervision is also required at the conclusion of a class suit. When an injunction class action has been litigated to a judgment, the court exercises discretion concerning the decree as in other injunction cases, explained in the preceding section. When a damages class suit has been litigated to a judgment, the court must supervise the allocation of the proceeds among the members of the class. In some instances, the defendant's illegal gain can be ascertained but not the identity of the victims—for example, where the judgment is for restitution of illegal profits in selling consumer products. In these instances, the court may nevertheless award judgment and distribute the award among a set of beneficiaries who approximate the original victims, a procedure called "fluid class" recovery. The court also must approve the fee to be paid the advocate for the class. Similar supervision is exercised when a class suit is settled.

The class suit remains controversial. On the positive side, class suits facilitate claims by groups of individuals who otherwise could not enforce rights against a common wrongdoer. As such, they are a powerful legal corrective for wrongs committed in mass society. On the negative side, a class suit provides powerful leverage for a small group to assert rights of persons who may have no desire to be involved in litigation. The class suit procedure thus can be exploited by advocates interested in contingent fees and by social-action groups interested in legal coercion. Experience indicates that the class suit mechanism can accomplish its positive effects while being kept under reasonable control against its negative effects. In any event, there is little prospect that the class-action rules will be repealed.

In many circumstances a class suit is only formally different from other kinds of regulatory civil actions. Specifically, a "test case" or a regulatory civil action by a government agency often functions like a class suit. A test case by an individual who is in a situation similar to others establishes a legal precedent that applies not only to the individual but also to the others in the same situations. For example, a suit by an employee establishing his rights to pension benefits creates a precedent that benefits other employees; the employer's obligation to pay the benefit to all employers will be essentially the same as if the suit had been a class suit. Similarly, a regulatory civil action by a government agency can establish a legal obligation that directly benefits a group in much the same way as a class suit. However, the class suit allows a private party to take the initiative in bringing suit and also allows the cost of the suit to be spread among the beneficiaries.

Admiralty, Bankruptcy, Probate, and Divorce

Several forms of American civil procedure, in addition to suits for equitable remedies, resemble the civil law system in that juries generally are not employed. These include:

Admiralty. Admiralty proceedings arise from maritime activities such as ship charters and accidents at sea or on navigable inland rivers. These proceedings are within the exclusive competence of the federal courts.

Bankruptcy. Bankruptcy proceedings provide legal supervision of the financial affairs of businesses and individual debtors who are unable to meet their obligations. These proceedings are also within the exclusive competence of the federal courts.

Probate. Probate proceedings provide legal administration of decedents' estates. They are within the exclusive competence of the state courts.

Divorce and child custody. These proceedings adjudicate dissolution of marriage, legal separation of spouses, and allocation of property, financial support, and custody of children following divorce or legal separation. These are also within the exclusive competence of the state courts.

Each of these types of proceedings has its own specialized procedure, rooted in its own tradition. Historically, each originated in a specialized court in England whose procedure derived partly from the civil law tradition.

The ancient English Court of Admiralty had competence over legal disputes arising out of maritime activity, principally losses of ships and cargoes at sea. Adjustment of these losses required a proceeding in which all claimants and obligors were made parties. As a conceptual matter, the proceeding concerned the ship itself, as the subject of rights and duties on the part of the owners of the ship, shippers, captain and crew, and third parties. It thus is said that the proceeding is *in rem*—dealing with the ship as a thing. As a functional matter, the proceeding was designed to reconcile claims against the ship with ownership rights in the ship and its cargo. The proceeding compiled a schedule of assets, particularly the ship and its cargo if such remained, and a schedule of claims, including claims for lost cargo, unpaid charges owed to ship repairmen and suppliers, and the crew's unpaid wages and voyage shares. Upon verification of these assets and claims, the assets were sold and the proceeds disbursed among the claimants according to legal rules of priority.

Admiralty jurisdiction is a vital legal institution in maritime commerce. During the eighteenth century, the authority of the English admiralty court was extended to Great Britain's colonies, including those in America. In the brief period between outbreak of the Revolution in 1776 and adoption of the Constitution in 1787, the American state courts adjudicated maritime litigation, usually through adaptation of equity or common law procedure. The Constitution assigned admiralty jurisdiction to the federal courts, consistent with the general policy giving the federal government primary authority over matters of commerce, and the federal courts have exercised that jurisdiction ever since. By decision of the U.S. Supreme Court in the early nineteenth century, this authority was held to apply not only to the high seas but also to the country's vast inland lakes and rivers, notably the Great Lakes and the Mississippi.

Modern admiralty procedure is based on the federal rules of civil procedure. The rules of pleading and discovery are essentially the same, as is the procedure for trial and appeal. A substantial fraction of modern admiralty litigation involves personal injury to seamen and quayside workers. Most commercial disputes arising in maritime commerce are now resolved under arbitration agreements.

English bankruptcy procedure originated in merchant and borough courts of the premodern era, financial failure being an inherent aspect of mercantile trade. By the eighteenth century the Court of Chancery exercised some authority in cases of financial distress, particularly issuance of injunctions to restrain dissipation of assets by distressed debtors. In the same period American colonial courts exercised somewhat similar authority, which devolved to the state courts after the Revolution. The period between 1776 and 1787 in American history was one of severe financial hardship, in which there was strong political pressure to relieve debtors from their burdens. Creditors believed that state court proceedings allowed debtors too easily to escape their obligations.

Concern on the part of conservative financial interests inspired a provision in the Constitution giving Congress authority to establish a uniform bankruptcy law. However, after the Constitution's adoption, the debtor interest mobilized political resistance to implementation of this authority. Debtor insolvency proceedings accordingly were governed principally by state law until 1938. That year, in the wake of the Great Depression, Congress enacted a comprehensive statute regulating bankruptcy, on which modern bankruptcy procedure is based.

Bankruptcy procedure has two principal aspects. One consists of compiling the debtor's assets and liabilities with a view to selling the assets and disbursing the proceeds among claimants according to statutory priorities. Functionally, this aspect of bankruptcy procedure is like that in which admiralty deals with a ship loss. Like the admiralty proceeding, this aspect of bankruptcy is primarily administrative rather than adjudicative, being focused on organizing accounts rather than on resolving disputed legal contentions.

The other aspect of bankruptcy is adjudication of disputes about rights to assets in the debtor's possession and disputes about the debtor's obligations. Resolution of these disputes determines how the claimants will share in the assets. Adjudication of such disputes is conducted according to the general rules of civil procedure, in some instances including jury trial.

Judicial competence in matters of probate and divorce in England was vested in the church courts. Their procedure followed canon law and was similar to the civil law. The authority of the English church courts eroded after Henry VIII induced separation of the English church from Rome in the sixteenth century, and further eroded in the religious controversies involved in the English Revolution of the seventeenth century. However, the English church courts retained competence in probate matters, and probate tribunals based on this model were established in some of the American colonies. Competence in marital matters, or family law as it is now called, was similarly transplanted. However, divorce—as distinct from legal separation—remained generally unavailable until many years later. Probate and matters of family law remained within the authority of the states following the Revolution. Each state has its own procedure in both fields.

Probate is primarily a matter of administration rather than adjudication of disputes. The proceeding's primary function is to collect the decedent's assets, pay his debts, and distribute his property to his heirs. When litigation arises in connection with probate matters, the litigation usually is conducted not in the probate court but in the first-instance court of general competence, using the regular procedure of that court.

Divorce litigation until recent years involved issues of fault between the spouses, such as adultery, cruelty, and abandonment. This was because divorce traditionally could be obtained only by proof of such wrongs against the marriage. However, divorce now may usually be obtained at the initiative of either party without proof of fault—so-called "no-fault divorce." The issues in modern divorce proceedings therefore primarily concern allocation of property, postdivorce obligations of financial support between the former spouses, and custody and financial support for children. These matters are determined primarily by party negotiation. When negotiation fails and adjudication is necessary, it is conducted by the judge through procedure similar to that in other civil cases, but without a jury.

Admiralty, bankruptcy, probate, and divorce are similar in the following important respects: the proceedings concern accounting for assets and obligations; the judge has greater supervisory and administrative responsibilities than in ordinary civil litigation; and jury trial is not used except in adjudication of distinct legal claims incidental to these administrative functions. At the same time, they are similar to other civil proceedings in that the advocates play a central role in negotiation and administration; the same procedures of discovery generally apply; and the distinction is generally maintained between the pretrial and trial phases of litigation

Small Claims

Small claims is a procedure designed to permit ordinary citizens to bring claims for money with minimum legal formality. The procedure is administered in state trial courts, sometimes in a division that has limited monetary jurisdiction. Although the procedure is fairly simple, it is used less often by ordinary citizens than in debt collections by businesses and governmental agencies. However, the procedure at least reduces the litigation expenses that are charged against these debtors.

The ideal sought in small claims procedure is simplicity and efficiency without legal technicality. The complaint can be written in hand and need be only an informal narrative of the dispute. Summons is issued by the court, specifying a date when defendant must appear, whereupon the defendant may answer either in writing or orally, the procedure varying from state to state. There is no discovery stage, litigants being instructed to come to testify and to bring relevant documents to court. Trial is held by a judge without a jury and is conducted by informal conversation, the judge seeking to mediate as well as to adjudicate. The trial is usually scheduled for the same day as defendant appears in court, although the parties' uncertainty about how to conduct themselves often creates a necessity for a second hearing. A judgment for the plaintiff is an award of money. No statement of reasons is required, although many judges make such a statement orally.

In many small communities the procedure works much as intended. In larger cities, however, the court's operation is often hurried, hasty, and conducted amid confusion. Litigants are often angry when they are not given their due as they see it, and judges are often exasperated by the parties' unrealistic expectations. Furthermore, the court provides little assistance in collecting its judgments, a task the winner must undertake for himself. The small claims court is therefore rarely attractive to the ordinary citizen, who typically abandons a legal claim of modest amount rather than trying to enforce it.

Organizations that have many debts to collect use small claims procedure because it is simple and inexpensive and can be managed without hiring an advocate. Accordingly, small claims procedure is put to greatest use by sellers of consumer goods and moneylenders. In some localities it is also used by tax-collecting authorities and by hospitals and medical services to collect unpaid bills. These cases are rarely contested, so judgment is by default. The debt collectors benefit from the speed of the proceedings; the debtors' benefit to the extent that their obligation for costs is minimized.

A few cities have similar courts to deal with landlord-tenant disputes. Where landlord-tenant courts exist, they function much like small claims courts; most claims are by landlords for unpaid rent and most result in default judgment.

The ideal of the small claims procedure has never been realized, for reasons that both the legal system and society are reluctant to face. A basic cause is that most legal disputes involving ordinary citizens arise from failure to pay money. In many cases the failure to pay may be justified, for example, because goods sold were of poor quality. However, a common underlying problem is financial overcommitment by the debtor, since many American families are chronically in debt. It is apparently contrary to American political mores that the government should intervene with debt-management service in private affairs. Moreover, while ordinary American citizens readily talk about their legal rights, they shy at the aggression, uncertainty, and possible humiliation of trying to enforce those rights. These tendencies may explain not only why small claims procedure fails to achieve its objectives, but also why Americans rely heavily on lawyers, who carry the burdens of controversy for them.

Alternative Dispute Resolution

The complexity, technicality, and expense of American litigation inspire repeated calls for some better way of resolving legal disputes. One effort has been reform of civil procedure itself, first through the code pleading system and more recently through the Federal Rules. However, each of these systems has facilitated litigation as much as it has simplified or impeded it. Hence, the volume, scope, and intensity of litigation have not abated. Another effort has been the search for procedures other than litigation to resolve legal disputes. Procedures of this kind are called Alternative Dispute Resolution, or ADR for short.

ADR procedures have two legal foundations. One is the court system. Here, the procedures are linked to court procedures at one stage or another. Sometimes these are called "court-annexed ADR procedures," in recognition of their connection to the courts. These are described in chapter 6. The other legal foundation of ADR procedure is a contractual or indirect contractual relationship between the parties, of which the basic model is arbitration. Arbitration may be required in a contract between specific parties or in a contract by an association of which the parties are members—for example, arbitration of employee-manager disputes in a labor-management agreement.

Voluntary submission to ADR after a dispute has arisen is inhibited by the party incentives occurring at that stage. In principle, every person is entitled to resort to litigation to assert or defend legal rights. When a legal dispute arises, one party is usually in a more favorable strategic position—that is, a position in which the status quo is more advantageous than undergoing the risk of an adverse determination by an impartial authority. That party ordinarily has little incentive to submit to such an authority, unless it is under legal compulsion to do so or it is concerned that its reputation or relationship with third parties will be jeopardized by intransigence. Except where such reputational considerations lead the stronger party to submit to an ADR procedure, compulsion is usually required to overcome the stronger party's insistence on the status quo. The court can compel parties to submit to ADR procedures when a dispute has already come to court or when an arbitration procedure has previously been stipulated by contract. Otherwise, ADR usually depends on mutual good will of the parties.

The need for legal compulsion to resolve serious disputes is perhaps greater in American society than in others. Institutions based on traditional authority are relatively weak in the United States: for example, the church, government agencies such as the police, village elders, and business proprietors. Hence, conflict is not easily channeled and resolved through such relationships. In default of these alternatives, conflict is articulated in terms of the authority of law and rights recognized by law. Conflict expressed in these terms not only invokes the authority of courts but also implicitly rejects other authority.

The paucity of tradition-based authority structures in the United States explains the paradox of American ADR. The weakness of tradition-based authority generates strongly felt social need for ways to resolve interpersonal and intergroup conflicts without the cost, delay, acrimony, and depersonalization of litigation. Hence, there is strong and sometimes plaintive desire to avoid litigation through effective ADR procedures. By the same token, however, the absence of nonlegal authority structures leaves no ground in which to anchor ADR procedures. For example, neighborhood mediation has been tried in inner cities, but the disputing parties rarely have common allegiance to a nonlegal authority that they both recognize. The same is generally true of landlord-tenant relations in public housing projects in which ADR has been tried, and in relationships between businesses. Unless the parties in a dispute are bound by a preexisting contract for arbitration or mediation, they usually either work out their differences by negotiation, let their differences remain unresolved, or look to litigation. The idea of yielding to some other authority appears to be alien and frightening.

ADR procedures as they exist are essentially of two kinds, mediation and arbitration. Mediation consists of discussion, exploration, and persuasion by a third party in whose disinterestedness the parties have confidence. Its aim is to facilitate a negotiated agreement. Mediation is usually most effective when it is conducted under threat that a compulsory procedure will be activated if mediation fails. Hence, court-supervised mediation, including settlement discussions under the court's own supervision, is widely employed.

On the same basis, various forms of arbitration are conducted under court sponsorship. In one form, after the parties have conducted discovery, a trial is held before a three-member panel of arbitrators instead of a single judge or a jury. Another form of court-annexed ADR consists of presenting the evidence to an unofficial jury, which then gives its reaction—leading (it is hoped) the parties to revise their positions concerning settlement. Still another is "rent-a-judge," whereby the parties employ their own judge and try the case according to the usual trial rules. This procedure, usually employing retired trial judges, is now commonly used in commercial litigation in major urban centers. For many years the courts were apathetic or antagonistic to ADR procedures, regarding them as affording "second-class justice." The courts have come to recognize, however, that although channeling cases into "mini-trials" or arbitration may result in second-class justice, available second-class justice is better than unavailable first-class justice. The same is true for arbitration required by contract, which usually affords better justice than a prohibitively expensive right to litigate.

CHAPTER NINE

Jurisdiction, Appeal, and Final Judgment

A court must have subject matter jurisdiction to render judgment in a case brought before it. That is, the fundamental law establishing the court system—the constitution and implementing statutes—must have conferred authority on the court to determine cases of the type in the pending action. In American terminology, this authority is called "subject matter jurisdiction," while in other legal systems it is called "competence." There is an additional problem concerning the authority of a court located in one state to adjudicate a case involving persons or transactions located outside its borders. This matter is commonly called territorial jurisdiction.

Even when the trial court has jurisdiction, the legal correctness of its judgment may be questioned on appeal. Broadly speaking, an appeal may challenge the procedural regularity of the trial, the correctness of the legal principles applied there, the sufficiency of the evidence to establish liability, or all of these aspects of the proceeding. In American procedure an appeal is considered a separate proceeding rather than a continuation of the first-instance trial, and it is governed by a distinct body of rules of appellate procedure.

After all avenues of appeal have been pursued, the judgment ordinarily is a conclusive determination of the legal dispute. A valid final judgment precludes relitigation of the claim presented in the litigation, and also precludes relitigation of claims that could have been asserted concerning the transaction or incident in question. This effect of a judgment is called claim preclusion or *res judicata*.

The judgment also precludes relitigation of issues actually adjudicated. This effect of a judgment is called issue preclusion or collateral estoppel.

If the court rendering the judgment lacked jurisdiction, the judgment may be held to be invalid. An invalid judgment does not conclude the dispute, and the parties may renew litigation through another proceeding. In certain circumstances a separate proceeding may be brought to challenge the validity of a prior judgment. Such a proceeding is called a collateral attack, meaning that the judgment is being challenged in a suit that is "beside" or collateral to the original proceeding.

The rules governing these matters are relatively technical and they have relatively infrequent application in practice. However, the questions of judicial authority they address go to the very foundation of the judicial system. From the viewpoint of judges and lawyers, the rules governing these matters are important "lawyers' law."

Challenging Subject Matter Jurisdiction

The plaintiff selects the court in which the litigation is commenced, ordinarily the court of the state where the incident occurred. Implicit in this selection is the plaintiff's assumption that the court has competence of the action. If the defendant responds by addressing the merits of the plaintiff's claim, the defendant implicitly recognizes the court's authority. The plaintiff rarely has any incentive to bring an action in a court that lacks subject matter jurisdiction, for doing so would only delay opportunity to obtain an adjudication on the merits. Hence, the plaintiff's choice of forum is usually correct.

However, plaintiff may have brought the action in a court whose authority is legally questionable. The competence of the court could depend on facts of which the plaintiff was uncertain, for example, the place of the defendant's residence. Similarly, in an action brought in federal court and purportedly based on federal law, the federal court may determine that the action does not arise from federal law; the action would have to be dismissed for lack of subject matter jurisdiction.

Objection to subject matter jurisdiction normally is made by defendant at the initial stage of the action, by a motion to dismiss the action. If the motion is granted, the suit is terminated, unless upon an appeal from the dismissal the appellate court reinstates the proceeding. If the motion is denied, the suit proceeds to the merits. However, the defendant may make objection to the court's subject matter jurisdiction even after responding on the merits. Furthermore, the court may question its competence on its own motion, that is, without objection having been made by a party.

Preliminary Attack on Territorial Jurisdiction

As discussed in chapter 2, the American constitutional system is a federation in which each state is quasisovereign and as such has its own court system. A corollary of this legal structure is that the courts of a given state have authority to adjudicate all civil controversies between persons and organizations located in that state, except litigation exclusively reserved to the federal courts. They also have authority to adjudicate controversies concerning property located in that state. Furthermore, they have authority to adjudicate controversies involving persons and organizations residing elsewhere when the transaction occurred within the state or was otherwise significantly related to it.

The rules governing these matters are called the rules of state court territorial jurisdiction. They generally correspond to similar rules in international law; for jurisdictional purposes, the states are like national states in the international community. According to this concept, each state has authority to adjudicate civil controversies arising within its territory. The concept also implies that a state's courts do not have authority to compel a resident of another state to respond concerning litigation unrelated to the state asserting jurisdiction. The law of state court territorial jurisdiction is thus a species of international law that operates within the American federal system.

The "international" character of these rules is, however, controlled by the U.S. Constitution. As discussed in chapter 7, the Constitution guarantees citizens of each state access to the courts of other states on equal terms with citizens of the latter. The Constitution also requires each state to recognize and give effect to the judgments rendered by courts of other states. Directly relevant to territorial jurisdiction, the Due Process Clause of the Fourteenth Amendment prohibits a state court from exercising judicial authority over persons and organizations that are not situated in the state and have not been involved in transactions that occurred there. The logic of the due process requirement is as follows: state courts may not impose judgment without due process of law; due process of law contemplates that a tribunal purporting to adjudicate a controversy should have valid legal authority to do so; a state court does not have valid legal authority to compel response by a person or organization located outside its boundaries, unless the transaction sued on occurred within the state or is otherwise significantly related to the state; therefore, a judgment rendered by a court lacking legal authority is legally invalid.

However, it is established that a state court may properly exercise authority over a nonresident who consents to the court's jurisdiction. Such consent may be express or implied. Consent to jurisdiction is conclusively implied if a defendant responds to the court without making objection to its territorial jurisdiction. Thus, if a defendant fails to make such an objection in its first response to the court, the objection may not be made thereafter. This is an important technical distinction from objection to subject matter jurisdiction, which may be made after responding on the merits.

A defendant wishing to challenge the court's territorial jurisdiction has an alternative way of doing so, but one that involves serious legal risk. Instead of responding in the court where the action is brought, the defendant may refuse to appear in that court and thereby permit default judgment to be entered against him or her.

When effort is thereafter made to enforce the judgment, the defendant then opposes enforcement on the ground that the judgment is invalid. Such a maneuver is a collateral attack, discussed below. If the defendant is successful in this attack, both the enforcement procedure and the original judgment are declared void. However, the defendant's motion will be denied if the court in the enforcement proceeding concludes that the court rendering the original judgment had proper territorial jurisdiction. When the motion is denied, it signifies that the judgment is valid, and that in turn implies that the judgment is conclusive in favor of the plaintiff. Thus, by delaying attack on territorial jurisdiction, the defendant waives any right to contest the merits of the plaintiff's claim. The defendant's whole position stands or falls on the question of territorial jurisdiction, a risky strategy.

Historically, the scope of state court territorial jurisdiction was confined to persons and organizations physically located within the state. In the days before modern transportation and communication, this definition of territorial jurisdiction rarely imposed serious inconvenience, because litigation occurred between residents of the same locality. With the development of modern interstate transportation and communication, however, personal and business transactions cross state lines every day as a matter of course. The limitations on state court territorial jurisdiction have been correspondingly relaxed. The modern rule, based on the Due Process Clause, is that a state may exercise territorial jurisdiction over persons and organizations located outside its boundaries if the state had "minimum contacts" with the transaction involved in the litigation. For example, if a New York motorist is involved in a traffic accident while driving in Texas, that motorist may be sued in the Texas courts by a person injured in the accident. So also, a business based in Florida that does business in California may be sued in the California courts in disputes arising from those transactions. The concept of minimum contacts is technically complicated in many specific applications, but the basic concept is simple. Through this adaptation of the due process requirement, the territorial scope of the state courts' authority generally accords with practical convenience in their administration of civil justice.

By a peculiar historical evolution, the territorial limitations on the authority of state courts also govern most cases in the federal district courts. As discussed in chapter 3, in creating the federal courts in 1789, Congress provided that each federal district court should use the forms of process employed by the courts of the state in which the federal court sat. This provision has been interpreted to mean that the territorial jurisdiction limitations on state courts should also apply to the federal courts. For example, if a case is brought in the federal district court in New York against a citizen of Connecticut, the defendant cannot be required to respond unless either he or she is served with summons while in New York, or the transaction involved in the suit had some significant connection with New York. However, federal statutes make this limitation inapplicable in specified types of federal litigation; in these cases, the territorial jurisdiction of a federal district court extends to the whole country.

The procedure for challenging the territorial jurisdiction of a federal first-instance court is essentially the same as that for such a challenge in state court.

Appeal from Final Judgment

After a trial court judgment an aggrieved party may appeal. The concept of "aggrieved party" includes a defendant against whom judgment has been awarded, a plaintiff who has been denied recovery, and a plaintiff awarded a smaller recovery than sought in the plaintiff's claim.

In general, appeal make be taken only when the proceedings in the trial court have been concluded in a final judgment. This is known as the "final judgment rule." Hence, a ruling prior to final judgment may not be appealed at the time the ruling was made. Instead, such a ruling may be reviewed by the appellate court only if appeal is subsequently taken from the final judgment. Exceptions to the final judgment rule are discussed below.

An appeal is considered a separate proceeding whose purpose is to review the regularity of the trial court proceeding. Appellate review is guided by three general principles. First, the appellate court ordinarily will not reconsider issues of fact determined in the court of first instance. This limitation derives principally from the position of the jury as the finder of fact; it is beyond the authority of the court to redetermine the jury's verdict except to the limited extent of considering whether the evidence was sufficient for a rational verdict. There is similar deference to findings of fact by a judge in cases tried without a jury. Appellate courts do not wish to "retry the case," and they also recognize that the trial judge is in a better position to evaluate the credibility of witnesses.

The second general principle of appellate review is that the appellate court has complete authority to reconsider questions of law determined in the trial court. This authority extends to matters of procedure as well as to substantive legal issues. For example, the appellate court can consider whether the trial judge erred in applying the rules of evidence or in limiting the scope of discovery in the pretrial phase. The contrast between the appellate court's general authority concerning questions of law, and its very limited authority concerning questions of fact, makes the distinction between "fact" and "law" crucial in an appeal. Although that distinction is fundamental in principle and receives endless analytical and jurisprudential refinement, it remains artificial in marginal application.

The third principle is that the appellate court's responsibility is to determine whether the judgment in the lower court was erroneous in a significant way, not whether it was completely correct or just in result. It is recognized that a trial is a largely extemporaneous event in which incidents occur suddenly and unexpectedly, to which the trial judge must respond quickly. It is also recognized that trial judges vary widely in their practical skill, legal ability, and powers of concentration. It is held that the trial judge has broad "judicial discretion" in many matters—for example, in the admission of evidence and the terms in which the jury is instructed. It is also held that "harmless error" is not a basis for reversal. "Harmless error" describes mistakes that, in the appellate court's estimate, had no substantial prejudicial effect on the rights of the parties.

Appellate procedure, like that in the trial courts, is based on the adversary system. The advocate for the appellant must organize the record on appeal and present arguments for reversing or modifying the judgment of the court below. The appellate court is required to consider only those issues that the parties submit in their briefs, although it is has authority to reverse or modify on the basis of its own analysis of the record. This authority is often exercised in criminal cases, especially where the defendant appears to have been inadequately represented, but it is rarely exercised in civil cases.

Appellate procedure varies in detail from one state to another and in the federal courts is regulated by the Federal Rules of Appellate Procedure. Under typical rules, an aggrieved party commences the appeal by filing a notice of appeal, identifying the judgment from which appeal is taken, the court to which appeal is made, and the opposing parties to the appeal. The notice must be filed within a fixed time after entry of the judgment, usually thirty days.

The record on appeal consists of documents specified by the appellant, augmented by those designated by the respondent. Except in extraordinary circumstances, the appellate court will not consider any other evidence concerning the proceedings in the first instance-court. The record on appeal ordinarily will include the pleadings, motions, and orders before trial, and a verbatim transcript of the oral proceedings at trial. These proceedings will have been recorded as they occurred by a court reporter, who employs stenography or audio recording or a combination of these techniques. The trial judge does not prepare a summary of the evidence, as is the practice in the civil law system. The discovery depositions and other discovery material usually are not included in the record on appeal, except such part as was introduced as evidence at trial.

The record of evidence in an American appeal contrasts sharply with that presented to the court in a second-instance proceeding in the civil law system. In the civil law the trial judge prepares a recital of the testimony that condenses the evidence into conclusory form, thus overlaying the original evidence with the judge's interpretation. The record in an American appeal includes the questioning and interchanges of the advocates, the testimony of the witnesses, and the rulings of the judge in full, unrefined form. This gives the appellate judges as complete a picture of the factual aspects of the case as if they could take additional testimony, as may be done in the civil law system. This in turn allows the advocates to invite the appellate court to impose its analysis on the case. Thus, the American appellate court has less need to receive new evidence because it has a record containing all the evidence the parties wanted to present.

The parties' legal arguments are presented in written appellate briefs. The appellant's brief is filed first, then respondent's, and then a reply brief by appellant. An appellant's brief describes the proceedings and judgment in the court, the key facts, and the appellant's argument. The format of the respondent's brief is essentially similar.

The summary of an appellant's argument could be as follows:

I. The Trial Court Lacked Subject Matter Jurisdiction of This Case and Erred in Failing to Dismiss the Action on That Basis.
   A. The Court's Jurisdiction Is Limited to Matters in Which the Amount in Controversy Exceeds $50,000.
   B. Although the Complaint Alleged Damages of $100,000, the Evidence Supporting Defendant's Motion to Dismiss Shows That Recovery Could Not Legally Exceed $35,000.

II. The Trial Court Erred in Admitting Evidence of Consequential Losses Suffered by Plaintiff by Reason of Defendant's Breach of Contract.

A. Damages for Breach of Contract Are Only Those Directly Resulting from Defendant's Breach. Such Damages Do Not Include Inconvenience Suffered by the Party against Whom the Breach was Committed.

B. The Trial Court Admitted Evidence of Inconvenience Suffered by Plaintiff, Resulting in an Excessive Verdict.

The briefs may not exceed specified page limits, typically thirty typed, double-spaced pages, except by special permission from the appellate court. In multiparty cases, each appellant and each respondent is permitted to submit its own brief.

After the briefs are submitted, the parties may be permitted oral argument. In times past, extensive oral argument was customary: some early cases in the U.S. Supreme Court were argued for several days on each side. Today, oral argument is usually limited to fifteen minutes per side, and in some appellate courts oral argument is permitted only in especially complicated cases. Oral argument in modern procedure is relatively informal. The judges often interrupt with questions seeking clarification of important points, and counsel are expected to reply extemporaneously. When the oral argument is concluded, the court takes the case under consideration. Only in rare emergencies is the appellate court's judgment announced immediately.

In the U.S. Supreme Court, all nine justices participate in all cases unless excused on account of illness or some other special reason. The state supreme courts generally follow the same practice, although some of them hear some appeals in panels of three or four. Intermediate appellate courts normally hear appeals in panels of three judges. In cases of unusual importance, an appellate court that usually sits in panels may sit as a whole. This is called an en banc hearing, meaning that the entire bench is participating.

The appellate court reaches its decision by majority vote among the judges participating. Most decisions are unanimous. The decision is usually presented in a written opinion setting forth the facts and the court's legal analysis. The opinion is prepared by one of the participating judges, assignments of this task being made by rotation or by the judge presiding over the panel. Appellate judges have legal assistants called law clerks, who are usually recent graduates of law schools engaged in a one-year apprenticeship. The law clerks bring with them fresh viewpoints of the law, often informed by current scholarship at the law schools. Their influence moderates the isolation in which appellate judges work and has some indeterminable effect on judicial decisions, perhaps only on the erudition in rhetoric and citation.

Most appellate court opinions speak for all the participating judges. Dissenting opinions are freely permitted, and often are rendered in controversial cases. The decisions of appellate courts are printed in bound volumes, issued in chronological series, and become precedent in future cases.

After the appellate court has rendered its decision, the parties have a short period in which they may apply for reconsideration. However, petitions for reconsideration are rarely granted and, accordingly, are infrequently made by the advocates.

If the appellate decision has been rendered by an intermediate appellate court, a party aggrieved by that court's decision may petition to take a further appeal to the highest court. Thus, a party aggrieved by the decision of a federal circuit court of appeals may make such a petition to the U.S. Supreme Court; a party aggrieved by the decision of a state intermediate appellate court may make such a petition to the supreme court of that state. These petitions are granted only in the discretion of the court to which they are presented. The highest court's discretion generally is exercised on the basis of the general importance of the legal questions involved in the appeal and the public importance of the specific case. Only a small fraction of appeals decided by intermediate appellate courts are accepted for a second appeal.

An appellate court's decision is accompanied by a directive for disposition of the case, called the court's mandate. The mandate directs that the judgment of the court below be affirmed, that it be modified (for example, by changing the damages awarded), or that it be reversed in whole or in part. Technically, the final judgment to be entered in the case is that of the trial court; the appellate court's mandate is simply an order concerning the terms that the judgment should express.

Appellate review serves several functions. First, it is a means by which a party can overcome error in the case, whether the error is procedural unfairness, the failure of the trial court to apply appropriate legal principles in reaching decision, or the rendition of judgment on the basis of legally insufficient evidence. This is the corrective function of appellate review. Second, appellate review is a means of monitoring the performance of the first-instance courts, making them continually aware that their performance is under scrutiny by higher judicial authority. This is a supervisory function. Third, the decisions of appellate courts expound and reformulate the law, thus providing specific legal guidance concerning similar transactions in the future. Under the theory of precedent, a prior decision of a court of equal or superior authority is accorded presumptive authority in a subsequent similar case. That is, precedent should be followed unless there is good reason for departing from it. Good reason, however, includes the courts' evolving sense of appropriate public policy, which changes over the course of time. Finally, the exercise of all the foregoing powers constitutes an authoritative voice in the governance of the community.

The structure of the appellate system affects the judiciary's lawmaking function. That of the federal court system—trial court, intermediate appellate court for ordinary appeal, discretionary jurisdiction by the highest court—is now replicated in almost all the states. The task of supervising trial court adjudication is performed primarily by the intermediate appellate courts in the grist of hundreds of more or less routine appeals each year. The highest courts decide relatively few cases, chosen for their importance and briefed, argued, and decided with primary attention to legal issues of general significance. Having such an agenda makes the highest court an office of incremental law reform, in various directions. It falls to the lower courts to apply the resulting pronouncements and to work out their implications. The functions of a supreme court, in the states as well as in the federal system, thus more closely approximate those of the legislative, facing forward as lawgivers. The functions of intermediate appellate courts more closely approximate the traditional conception that courts find law established in the past.

The published opinions of American appellate courts number several thousand each year. In a populous state such as California, New York, or Texas, there are hundreds of such decisions each year. Over time, more than a hundred thousand published American judicial decisions have accumulated, any one of which in principle may be relevant as precedent. The size and complexity of this body of documentation has led to highly sophisticated cataloguing systems. Appellate court decisions today are recorded verbatim in computer storage and may be retrieved by anyone equipped with computer access. The same computerized system is used to search statutes, regulations, professional periodicals, and scholarly law journals.

The flow of published decisions is continuously reintegrated into existing law. This is accomplished not only by the courts' reliance on them as precedent, but by professional and scholarly commentary. There are hundreds of legal journals, law reviews, legal newspapers, specialized newsletters, updating services, treatises, and continuing legal education briefing books. This legal information system continuously scans new legislation, judicial decisions, regulations, and other legal events; identifies new developments in various legal fields; and annotates existing legal sources with the changes. The aim is to provide a current "snapshot" of a relentless flow of legal information. The decisions of the courts contribute to the flow and are shaped by it.

Appeals to the Supreme Court of the United States

Almost all cases considered by the present-day Supreme Court of the United States come before the Court through exercise of its discretion. There are five procedures by which a case can come to the court; one of these takes the form of a suit commenced directly in the Supreme Court and the others are appeals.

First, in a very limited category of disputes, a claim may be brought directly in the Supreme Court under authority called the court's "original jurisdiction." In practice, the Court appoints a special judicial officer in these cases to take evidence and make preliminary findings of fact and conclusions of law, which then form the basis of the Court's consideration of the issues. Notable in this category are suits between states—for example, over state boundaries—and suits in which ambassadors for other nations are directly involved. Perhaps one or two cases a year are presented to the Court on this basis.

Second, in another very limited category of cases originating in the lower federal courts, an appeal may be taken directly to the Supreme Court. At one time this was possible in many constitutional cases, but in modern times such "direct appeal" is limited to certain cases involving reapportionment of state legislative electoral districts.

Third, in a case pending in a federal court of appeals, that court is authorized to certify a question of importance to the Supreme Court in order to obtain an authoritative ruling on the question. In practice this provision is rarely used, it being recognized by the lower courts that the Supreme Court should determine which cases it will decide.

Fourth, when final judgment has been rendered in one of the federal courts of appeals, the losing party may petition the Supreme Court to consider the case. The procedure is called a petition for a writ of certiorari, a term of ancient common law usage meaning "bring forth the record."

Last, when final judgment has been rendered in a state court involving a question of federal law, and all appeals within that state's court system have been exhausted, the losing party may petition the Supreme Court to consider the federal issues involved in the case. This procedure is also a petition for certiorari. If the petition is granted, the record in the state court is brought up as the basis of the Court's consideration of the case; if the petition is denied, the state court's judgment is final. Until modern times, some cases within this category could be taken to the Supreme Court by appeal of right. However, these appeals now rest within the Court's discretion.

The number of petitions to the Court has slowly increased over history to six or seven thousand per year. Much of the Court's attention is devoted to deciding which cases to accept. By established practice, the Court grants a petition if four of its members vote to do so. In this way, a majority cannot prevent consideration of an issue they might prefer to avoid. An important part of the Court's institutional strategy is its selection of cases. Often the Court tries to defer consideration of a major legal issue until it has been decided by several different lower courts, thus giving the Court a more complete view of the problem and its ramifications.

A petition for certiorari is prepared by the advocate for the party. It is a short document, not more than thirty printed pages, describing the significant legal issues presented, the facts of the case, and the importance of the issues. The opposing party may file a brief urging rejection of the petition, for example, contending that the facts are not as stated in the petition or that a significant legal issue is not actually involved. The Court's decision whether to accept the case is usually based on these documents, although the Court has authority to request additional documentation. A high degree of skill is required in preparing a petition, for it must be short, clear, and persuasive.

If a petition is granted, then a record is prepared of the proceedings in the court below and the parties submit written briefs as in other appeals. Oral argument is usually granted, one half-hour on each side, but the Court decides many cases solely on the briefs.

The Court hears arguments from early in the fall of each year until the late spring and completes its annual term by the end of June. Each week during the year it has a private decision conference in which the justices express their views and cast preliminary votes.

The writing of the Court's opinion is assigned by the Chief Justice, unless he or she dissents from the conclusion, in which event assignment of the opinion is made by the senior justice in the majority. An opinion is circulated in draft among the justices and is often revised on the basis of responsive comment and discussion. Many opinions are unanimous, but dissenting opinions are often given in highly controversial cases. The final opinions, both majority and dissents, are public documents and are printed in chronological series. Thus, the decision in *United States v. Nixon,* for example, has a citation as follows: 418 U.S. 683 (1974). This means that the decision is in volume 418 of the series *United States Reports,* beginning at page 683 of that volume, and that the decision was rendered in 1974.

Generally speaking, similar procedure and decisional process is employed in discretionary appeal to the highest court of the state within the state court systems.

Interlocutory Appeal

As noted above, the final judgment rule postpones opportunity to appeal until final decision in the trial court even when important matters have been determined in the pretrial stage. However, where the trial judge commits a serious error at an early stage of the litigation, postponement of appeal often results in serious injustice. Unless immediate appellate review can be obtained, the remaining phases of the case may be entirely useless effort. The risk of such consequences can be avoided by "interlocutory" appellate review, meaning review while deliberations are still proceeding in the court below.

Various kinds of rulings can justify interlocutory appellate review. For example, if the trial judge overrules an objection to the court's jurisdiction, the proceedings in the trial court go forward, possibly through a full-scale trial. On subsequent appeal from the final judgment, the appellate court may decide that the objection to jurisdiction should have been sustained; on this basis, the trial on the merits will have gone for nothing.

A similar problem can arise when privileged evidence is involved. If the trial judge sustains a claim of privilege—for example, communications between attorney and client—vital evidence may thereby be excluded. If upon appeal from the final judgment the communications are held not to be privileged, the appellate court may also be compelled to order a new trial because the evidence was withheld. On the other hand, if the judge overruled an objection to privileged communications, the receipt of that evidence may later be held on appeal to have contaminated the trial. Again a new trial would be required that could have been avoided if interlocutory appeal had been available.

These practical considerations become especially pressing when a jury trial is involved. Jury trials are generally more time-consuming than trials to judges without juries, so that greater waste of effort is at risk. Furthermore, errors in admission of evidence in a jury trial are more likely to be considered prejudicial than those in a trial to a judge, whose decision may indicate whether he attached weight to the evidence whose admissibility is in dispute.

To deal with these problems, most states permit immediate appeal of an order that has strategic significance in the trial proceedings. Interlocutory appeal may also be permitted where the legal issue involved is of general importance, particularly procedural issues, such as ones concerning the scope of discovery. Although interlocutory appeal is now liberally allowed in most state court systems, the final judgment rule is more rigorously applied in the federal courts. In this respect federal procedure is less well adapted to modern litigation than its state counterparts.

The procedure in an interlocutory appeal generally corresponds to that in appeal from final judgment, except that it is streamlined. The record is usually much shorter, being only that portion of the trial proceedings necessary for consideration of the specific issue involved in the interlocutory appeal. For example, if the interlocutory appeal concerns the scope of discovery, the record may contain only the pleadings (which indicate the issues in the case), the terms of the discovery demand, and the objection to the demand. Such a record could be no more than twenty or thirty pages long. Not only is the record more abbreviated in an interlocutory appeal, but the schedule for briefs and argument is shorter. These economies reduce the interruption of the trial proceedings.

Interlocutory appellate review is almost always conducted before the intermediate appellate court, rather than before the state's highest court. The court's decision procedure—panels of three judges, decision by majority, written opinion that is usually unanimous—is essentially the same as in other appeals. The intermediate appellate court's decision is subject to further appeal to the highest court on the basis of the latter's discretion.

In some states, interlocutory appellate review is conducted through an "extraordinary writ" rather than an appeal. The extraordinary writs are *mandamus,* which is an order from the appellate court requiring the lower court to take specified action, and *prohibition,* which is an order requiring the lower court to refrain from specified action. The writs have their origin in ancient English common law, but have been adapted to facilitate interlocutory appellate review. The transformation of the ancient extraordinary writs is a classic legal fiction whereby new procedural wine has been put in old common law casks.

Invalid Judgments

It is a universal principle of law that a judgment is a conclusive determination of the legal controversy to which it is addressed. This principle, known generically as that of res judicata, is explained in the following section. Broadly speaking, a valid judgment is conclusive even if subsequently revealed evidence shows that the judgment was erroneous and therefore unjust. The principle of res judicata does not apply, however, if the judgment is invalid. There is great practical difference, therefore, between a valid judgment and one that is invalid.

Generally speaking, a judgment is invalid only if the court that rendered the judgment lacked jurisdiction or the proceeding was tainted by fraud. Other kinds of miscarriages of justice ordinarily do not invalidate a judgment—for example, the fact that the losing party's advocate was incompetent or that new evidence has been discovered that could lead to a different result. The validity of judgments is infrequently disputed, simply because most civil proceedings are conducted with approximate regularity.

A contention that a judgment is invalid can be pursued either in the court that rendered the judgment or in some other court. Ordinarily, resort must be made by a motion in the court that rendered the judgment. If the motion is granted, the judgment is invalidated and the original legal dispute is open for relitigation. Otherwise, the judgment remains in effect. The order resolving the attack on the judgment itself may be appealed like an ordinary appeal.

In some circumstances the judgment may come under attack in another court, as where the party who obtained the judgment seeks to enforce it in another court and in that court the losing party attacks the judgment's validity. For example, if the plaintiff obtained a judgment in California and sought to enforce it in New York to collect the money awarded, a special proceeding for this purpose is required in New York (see chapter 10). In the New York proceeding, the court must determine that the California judgment is valid before it will assist its enforcement. The defendant may oppose enforcement on the ground that the judgment is invalid, if there is a basis for doing so.

The judgment is presumed to be valid and the attacking party has the burden of proof to show otherwise. An attack based on lack of jurisdiction must show that the court had no authority to adjudicate the type of case involved, not merely that the court mistakenly exceeded its authority. Attack may similarly be based on the rendering court's lack of territorial jurisdiction.

An attack based on fraud must show that there was corruption involved, for example, bribery of the judge or the jury, or that there was substantial and deliberate use of evidence known to be fabricated. The law's reluctance to be more liberal in reopening the merits of a case often seems heartless. However, sad experience suggests that a claim that fraud was involved in the original proceeding sometimes is itself fraudulent or the product of embitterment at the result. It is unavoidable in the administration of justice that many cases are lost that might have been won, and therefore that many litigants are convinced they were denied justice. Some disappointed litigants continue to linger about courthouses and law offices, hoping that the face of justice will turn their way.

Res Judicata

Adjudication seeks both to do justice between the parties and to end their conflict. Once the procedure has done what it can by way of justice between the parties, the law does not permit the conflict to be reopened except in unusual circumstances. The governing concept is that of res judicata, which may be translated as "matter that has been decided."

The concept of res judicata is simple in principle: claims that were presented by the plaintiff, and the defenses interposed by the defendant, may not be relitigated. However, complications arise where the original proceeding did not actually address certain claims or defenses that might have been presented, or where other disputes have arisen that involve some of the same issues. The problem then is whether the original proceeding should close the door on matters beyond those it specifically addressed.

The traditional common law rule was that a judgment determined only the matters specifically addressed in the original litigation. This approach reflected the narrow scope of legal claims permitted under the writ system. In modern procedure the scope of res judicata corresponds to the enlarged scope of litigation afforded by modern rules of pleading, joinder, and discovery. As we have seen, a plaintiff now may present all plausible legal theories against virtually all potential defendants who may have contributed to plaintiff's loss, and through discovery explore all sources of evidence that might support these claims. Defendants have corresponding latitude concerning defenses and claims against third persons.

The scope of res judicata mirrors these opportunities. The rule is administered with the following questions in mind: Could the claim now being asserted in the subsequent case have been asserted in the first litigation? If the present claim could have been so asserted, is there any good reason why it should now be permitted? If the answer to the first question is affirmative, the answer to the second question is usually negative. The underlying policy is that one abundant opportunity to litigate should be sufficient.

A related rule is that of issue preclusion. The concept is that a party who has once litigated an issue against one party may not relitigate the issue against another party. For example, if a passenger in an automobile sues the driver, contending that the driver's carelessness resulted in injury to the passenger, and the passenger loses that claim, the passenger is precluded from making the same contention against the owner of the vehicle. The same principle generally applies to persons sued as defendants. For example, if a securities dealer is found liable for securities fraud in a civil suit by a government enforcement agency, the dealer may not dispute that issue in a subsequent suit brought by a victim of the fraud. The rule of issue preclusion gives substantial added effect to such civil enforcement actions. The same effect can result where a defendant is sued by several different claimants concerning the same wrong, for example, successive actions by passengers in a public transportation vehicle. In effect the first case, if won by the plaintiff, determines defendant's liability in all the similar cases. The rule of issue preclusion applies only to issues that were actually litigated, however.

An important limitation on the scope of claim and issue preclusion is that they do not apply against a person who has not personally litigated the matter. For example, if one passenger in a vehicle has lost an action claiming that the driver was negligent, this does not preclude another passenger from litigating that issue in a subsequent case against the driver. The underlying principle is that a party may not be precluded from asserting a legal claim without having a day in court. Thus, the rules of res judicata can operate asymmetrically. A defendant who loses against one of several claimants ordinarily is precluded from relitigating issues determined against him, but the other claimants ordinarily are not precluded from trying the issue anew. This relationship is an important factor in trial strategy and maneuver in situations involving multiple claimants.

As a practical matter, these ramifications of res judicata are usually resolved through settlement of claims. When a defendant has been successful against one plaintiff, other plaintiffs, even though they still have a right to a day in court, will usually lower their settlement expectations. However, the terms of settlement are determined in part by the estimates of the risk of loss by the parties' advocates, which in turn are affected by the rules of res judicata. The principle of res judicata therefore has effects in resolving legal disputes not only after judgment is rendered but also before a case goes to judgment.

CHAPTER TEN

Enforcement of Judgments

A judgment imposes an obligation on the person against whom it is rendered to perform according to its terms. Thus, a judgment for damages obliges the defendant to pay the amount specified; a judgment against a plaintiff usually involves an award of court costs that creates a similar obligation. However, the obligation created by a judgment is not self-enforcing, and the court does not provide enforcement on its own initiative. That initiative must be taken by the winning party if the judgment debtor does not voluntarily make payment. A judgment against an insolvent or recalcitrant opponent is often worthless, hence the term *judgment proof*.

A judgment for damages is enforced through procedures for seizing the judgment debtor's property and having it sold to provide funds to pay the judgment. The seizure is accomplished through a government official, usually the sheriff for state court judgments and the United States Marshal for federal judgments. The official acts on the basis of a court order, obtained by the judgment creditor, who must identify the property to be seized.

Movable property may be taken physically into custody by the enforcing officer. Intangible property—such as a bank account or shares of stock—may be "seized" through a court order, traditionally called a writ of garnishment, directing that the judgment creditor be recognized as having priority. Real property is seized by recording the judgment in the public land records.

The seizure does not itself transfer ownership to the judgment creditor. A further procedure is required consisting of a public sale called an execution sale. Requiring a public sale provides better assurance of realizing a fair price for the property, and it affords the judgment debtor one last opportunity to pay the judgment voluntarily, thus avoiding a forced sale. If the proceeds from the sale fail to cover the judgment, the judgment creditor can pursue other assets the debtor may have.

The procedure for enforcing a money judgment is complex and highly technical. Most states liberally immunize debtor property, such as the debtor's home and a vehicle required for employment. The exemption rules reflect sympathy for judgment debtors, who are imagined to be honest people being oppressed by rapacious creditors. Many judgment debtors are indeed victims of misfortune, but many others are people who have been irresponsible about their obligations. The complex procedural protections have paradoxical consequences. They make it difficult to enforce a judgment against a debtor who resists fulfilling his obligation to pay the judgment. They also impose high procedural costs against honest debtors. These difficulties have been mitigated in enforcement of family support following divorce, where the procedures have been substantially simplified. However, even in those proceedings the collection process is difficult and often unsuccessful. Further complications are involved when a judgment is entered in one state and the debtor's property is located in another.

The difficulties in enforcing money judgments are compounded by the liberal American bankruptcy law. This is particularly true of voluntary bankruptcy, whereby the debtor can obtain postponement and reduction of obligations. Similar liberality is given to businesses. When a debtor enters bankruptcy, proceedings to enforce judgments are suspended and allocation of the debtor's assets comes under control of the bankruptcy court.

These barriers to enforcement of money judgments significantly affect litigation strategy. There usually is no point in suing someone who has no assets. People who engage in risky activities are therefore often effectively immune from civil liability—for example, young male auto drivers who have minimum liability insurance, or none at all, or corporate managers who wreck their companies by incompetence or self-dealing. The losses caused by such malefactors fall on others. By the same token, there is great incentive to bring suit against persons and organizations with "deep pockets." The courts are aware of these realities and often have been inclined to adopt legal rules that will assure reparations for victims. As a consequence, there is pressure to expand the rules of legal liability to impose responsibility on parties with deep pockets, such as corporations, even if their responsibility is secondary.

For the same reason, liability insurance is highly significant in civil litigation strategy and practice. The insurance companies ordinarily pay judgments promptly and in cash. Discovery procedure permits a plaintiff to ascertain whether a defendant is insured, and also the scope and monetary extent of the insurance coverage. The facts about insurance coverage will influence which parties are brought in as defendants and, among parties joined, which are made the principal targets in presenting the evidence. Plaintiffs often seek to give lenient settlements to defendants who have little or no insurance, in expectation that freeing them from the case will result in testimony that is more favorable against the other defendants.

As a result of the difficulties with enforcement of judgments, the de facto immunity of wrongdoers who have no assets, and the significance of deep-pocket and insured defendants, civil litigation, although concerned with justice, usually begins and ends with consideration of money. This unpleasant truth is not readily accepted by people unfamiliar with litigation, but it is a fact of life for lawyers and the courts. That truth derives ultimately from the fact that justice in the real world is an expensive undertaking beset with great uncertainty.

Enforcement of Injunctions

As explained in chapter 7, an injunction is a judgment that orders the defendant to perform a specified act or to refrain from doing so. An injunction requiring an act is called a mandatory injunction; one requiring that an act not be done is called a prohibitory injunction. The problem then arises concerning the enforcement of an injunction. Since enforcement is often problematic, the court will take into account the feasibility of enforcement when it defines the terms of an injunction.

For many wrongs, money damages are the only practical remedy. This is true, for example, of physical injuries to persons and many intangible injuries. For business and commercial wrongs, it is generally simpler to calculate the resulting monetary loss than to specify a course of conduct that will make the plaintiff whole.

However, there are many kinds of wrongs for which money damages are not a suitable or sufficient remedy. One category is wrongful conduct that threatens to continue—for example, continuation of pollution, or wrongful use of trade secrets, or in marital disputes continuing harassment of a former spouse. Another category is injunctive relief in litigation aimed at the government, complaining that an agency either failed to provide legally required services or is carrying out governmental functions in an illegal way. In these and other types of cases, it may be evident that money damages would be difficult to calculate and perhaps difficult to collect and distribute. When the wrongful conduct is continuing, an injunction addressed to future conduct also can avoid future litigation to determine further damages.

The terms of an injunction are subject to broad discretion on the part of the trial judge. The court may simply order the defendant to desist from specified conduct. In most business and commercial litigation, an injunction to that effect is sufficient. Violation of an injunction can result in monetary penalties, which can be extremely high. A court may require financial security to guaranty performance of the injunction, or resort to other enforcement mechanisms. For example, it may require that the defendant make periodic reports of its conduct; that an independent inspector monitor the defendant's compliance; or that a trustee assume direct management of the activities covered by the injunction.

These techniques originally evolved in order to supervise the affairs of business corporations that were in financial difficulty.

They were widely used in the management of financially distressed railroads in the first half of the twentieth century and in bankruptcy proceedings involving other large corporations. They were adapted to the desegregation of public schools and to supervision of decrees concerning prisons, mental hospitals, and other public agencies. The remedial requirements in these cases are often comprehensive in scope, detailed in requirements, and extended in duration. Because they have involved supervision of public institutions, they have been called "institutional decrees."

Similar decrees have been used to supervise compliance with antitrust laws. A notable example is the decree that divided the American Telephone and Telegraph Company, which had been a single nationwide telecommunications system, into seven regional companies and a national long-distance telephone company. The decree imposed detailed restrictions on the business activities of the newly reorganized telephone companies, with the court retaining authority to modify the restrictions as changes developed in telecommunication technology and general economic conditions.

Decrees of such broad scope involve troublesome difficulties, however. The court becomes involved in complex and often politically controversial management functions in which judges are not trained and for which they lack supporting staff. Decrees governing public institutions such as schools often directly affect public finance, including taxation, which in turn involves the court in public budgetary disputes. The courts are in an especially sensitive position if the political organs of government are unsupportive, as has often been the case with institutional decrees requiring increased public expenditure.

It should not be supposed, however, that decrees of this kind are typical injunctions. Most injunctions involve small-scale private disputes over property or between business competitors, or they involve personal relationships, such as those between neighbors. In such cases, the decrees are simple and direct in their terms and are usually complied with voluntarily. Failure to comply can result in the defendant's being held in contempt of court, as discussed below.

Certain kinds of injunction decrees require no immediate administrative enforcement—for example, a decree canceling a contract or holding invalid a government regulation. Cancellation of a contract ordinarily does not require that the contract document be physically destroyed or impounded. Rather, the decree of cancellation gives the winning party legal immunity if the losing party attempts to enforce the contract in another lawsuit. The same effect can result from a decree correcting a mistake in property boundaries; the decree itself reconfigures the legal boundary, which then is the basis of future uses of the property.

A decree that requires no immediate enforcement is sometimes called self-executing. However, if the defendant refuses to abide by the decree, further judicial enforcement may be necessary. This perspective brings into focus the fact that injunction usually has effect because the loser voluntarily recognizes it. However, the decree itself cannot prevent an intransigent defendant from defiantly continuing his previous course of action. No legal judgment is self-executing in this sense. The courts remain dependent on the government's coercive powers, particularly those of the police. It was this kind of dependency that Alexander Hamilton contemplated when he observed that the judiciary is the "least dangerous branch" of government.

Specific Performance

Specific performance is a kind of injunction. The term refers to a decree that requires a party to a contract to perform obligations specified in the contract. Such a remedy may be appropriate where the contract calls for delivery of unique property or performance of unique services, the theory being that damages will be an inadequate remedy for the plaintiff's right to obtain the specific property. Hence, the remedy of specific performance reflects the general principle that an injunction may be awarded when a damages remedy will be inadequate. The classic case is an agreement to sell real property, such as a home, farm, or commercial building, but the principle applies to unique items such as a painting, sculpture, or antique automobile. Correlatively, specific performance is not awarded for breach of a contract to sell fungible movable property, for example, grain or mass-produced objects. A judgment for damages would provide money with which the plaintiff can buy equivalent goods in the market.

The principle of specific performance can be applied to performance of personal services. The classic case is a contract for a theatrical performance, such as that of a lead opera singer. Courts are understandably reluctant to compel personal conduct, especially since it might be impossible to assure good-faith performance. However, the result usually can be achieved indirectly. The star who refused to perform under a valid contract may be enjoined from performing for anyone else; since the compelled inactivity usually would be against the star's interest, compliance with the contract ordinarily would soon follow.

In modern times the courts remain reluctant to order directly the performance of personal service contracts such as employment agreements. Apart from the difficulty of assuring compliance is the consideration of personal freedom from legal servitude. Thus, money damages remains the primary remedy in such cases; however, the defendant may be enjoined from engaging in employment that competes with plaintiff.

Declaratory Judgments

A declaratory judgment is a judicial pronouncement of the rights of the parties, without an accompanying award of additional redress. For example, a court may declare that a business partnership has been dissolved, or that ownership of specific property is vested in one or the other of the parties, or that a contract remains in force despite the attempt of one of the parties to rescind it. A declaratory judgment thus transforms an uncertain legal relationship between the parties into one that is authoritatively defined.

No such remedy existed at common law or in equity, although

it was recognized in Scottish law. It was thought to require the court to engage in hypothetical speculation, a concern perhaps derived from the common law's original concern with wrongs involving actual violence. In any event, the common law courts traditionally would afford a remedy only when actual damage had been sustained; similarly, the courts of equity required a showing of immediate need for judicial intervention.

The concern to avoid hypothetical adjudication had constitutional significance in the American context. The American courts, as we have seen, are broadly engaged in making law in the course of deciding cases. This lawmaking function historically was constrained by the requirement that it be performed only in the course of deciding specific legal disputes—thus precluding gratuitous legal pronouncements, which would jeopardize the constitutional legitimacy of the courts. The requirement is often expressed by saying that the courts may give opinions only in deciding actual disputes and may not give advisory opinions. Because a declaratory judgment involves no reparation in the form of damages or an injunction, many legal analysts considered that declaratory judgments would involve the courts in inappropriate lawmaking through advisory opinions. These inhibitions were gradually overcome, it being recognized that traditional injunctive relief usually was declaratory in effect. Thus, it became accepted in this century that a declaratory judgment is an appropriate judicial function when the parties are in an actual dispute with imminent possibility of actual damage.

A declaratory judgment takes the form of a pronouncement of the parties' legal rights. For example, in a dispute concerning obligations under a contract, the court could specify the obligations or determine whether a required condition had been fulfilled. In many such proceedings the facts are undisputed, so that the court's task is to determine their legal implications. However, when factual disputes must be determined as a basis for a declaratory judgments, they are tried in the same way as other litigation, including the use of juries.

A declaratory judgment is conclusive of the legal and factual issues determined. It is expected that the judgment will guide the parties' subsequent behavior, as would an injunction. However, a declaratory judgment does not impose an immediate personal obligation enforceable by contempt of court. Hence, if a party fails to comply with a declaratory judgment, the injured party will request an injunction, directly requiring compliance. With this additional step, a declaratory judgment thus usually has the same practical effect as an injunction.

Contempt of Court

The ultimate judicial sanction is to hold a recalcitrant party in contempt of court. Contempt of court consists of refusal to obey a direct court order. Two different types of contempt sanction are recognized, although they are closely related: civil contempt commits the offending party to imprisonment, or conditionally imposes imprisonment or a money penalty, until the offender agrees to obey the court's order. The purpose is to coerce compliance. A judgment of criminal contempt commits the offending party to imprisonment, or imposes a money penalty, for the offense of having refused to comply. The purpose of criminal contempt is both to punish the immediate offender and to deter others from being disobedient to the courts.

A necessary predicate for either civil or criminal contempt is a direct order specifically requiring the party to perform or refrain from an act. The contempt sanction may be used whether the order is a mandatory injunction, requiring the defendant to perform an act, or a prohibitory injunction, requiring abstention from an act. It may be used to enforce not only final judgment injunctions but also temporary restraining orders, preliminary injunctions, and orders incidental to the administration of a trial. Thus, it may used to enforce an order requiring a party not to communicate with an opposing party except under the court's supervision, or a discovery order requiring disclosure of specified documents.

In contrast, a judgment for money damages is not enforceable by contempt of court. Such a judgment creates an obligation to pay the sum awarded and renders the judgment debtor's property liable to seizure and sale, as explained above. However, it is not a direct order to the judgment debtor, and hence cannot immediately be enforced by contempt. That the contempt power cannot be used to enforce a debt reflects the long-established policy against imprisonment for inability to pay a judgment debt. However, if the judgment debtor obstructs efforts to locate and sequester his property, the court may issue an injunction against continuing the obstruction. Such an injunction addresses the defendant's interference with enforcement of the judgment, not simply his or her failure to pay the judgment, and is enforceable through the contempt power, like any other injunction.

Neither civil nor criminal contempt may be imposed without compliance with further procedural safeguards. The party seeking the imposition of a contempt sanction must request the court for an "order to show cause," which requires the responding party to explain why he or she should not be found in contempt of court. An order to show cause may also be issued on the court's own motion. In response, the party charged may defend on the ground, for example, that he or she had not violated the order or that he or she was mistaken as to its terms. The validity of the original order may be challenged only if the order was clearly beyond the authority of the court.

The court's consideration of whether the order was violated and whether sanction should be imposed is called the "show cause hearing." It is conducted like an ordinary trial, except that pretrial discovery is permitted only in unusual circumstances. Often the prospect of a show cause hearing induces the responding party voluntarily to desist from violation. When the proceeding is for criminal contempt, it must be proved that respondent's violation was intentional, and the standard of proof is the same as in criminal cases—beyond a reasonable doubt. If a prison sentence is to be imposed, the respondent has a right to jury trial; there generally is no jury trial right in civil contempt proceedings.

The contempt power is essential to maintaining the courts' authority to determine a litigant's legal responsibilities. At the same time, its exercise is fraught with the risk of arbitrary exercise, especially if the judge becomes emotionally involved with the respondent's defiance. Advocates of due process argued that another judge always should be designated to determine contempt of court. However, such requirement could lead to infinite regress, in which the respondent becomes defiant in the contempt proceeding itself. In the extreme case, as in the incidents of ordinary litigation, therefore, the fairness of judicial procedure has to depend on the character and self-discipline of the judges and not merely on the rules of procedure.

CHAPTER ELEVEN

Perspectives of the American System

Modern American procedural law dates from the adoption of the Federal Rules of Civil Procedure in 1938. The older common law and code-pleading procedure had been criticized as unjust because, among other deficiencies, the plaintiff was given little access to evidence in the hands of a suspected wrongdoer. The Federal Rules radically simplified the pleading requirements imposed on plaintiffs and radically enlarged the opportunities by which one party could obtain evidence from an opposing party. Simplifying the pleading requirements has meant that a plaintiff can bring a civil action on the basis of strong suspicion, before obtaining fully substantiating evidence. Enlarging discovery has permitted both parties to develop proof by obtaining the records of the opposing party and by pretrial interrogation of witnesses, including the opposing party him- or herself.

Allowing all parties broader discovery has been on the whole of greater advantage to plaintiffs than to defendants. Plaintiffs have the burden of proof as to most issues and hence are the losers if evidence cannot be obtained. Furthermore, generally speaking, defendants have greater sources of private information than do plaintiffs. This results from the "natural selection" by which defendants are targeted by plaintiffs: a plaintiff in civil litigation wishes to collect money or redirect government power; money can be collected only from defendants who have money (or who have money enough to buy insurance), and redirection of government power requires suing a government agency; persons with money and government agencies usually have private compilations of relevant information, such as correspondence files and accounting records.

Energetic use of discovery procedure is encouraged by rules permitting generous damages and giving a share of the damages to plaintiff's lawyer through a contingent fee.

Other provisions of modern procedure are generally to the same effect. The rules concerning joinder of claims allow a plaintiff to proceed simultaneously against all potentially liable participants in the disputed transaction, on the basis of all plausible legal concepts. The class-action rule permits a group to organize for prosecution of many relatively small claims against a common adversary. The rules concerning joinder of parties allow the plaintiffs injured in the same transaction to act together in prosecuting suit.

The Federal Rules therefore changed the strategic balance between claimants and defendants compared with that under the previous procedural system. They are relatively advantageous to individuals as against organizations such as corporations; to citizens as against the government; and to the have-nots as against the wealthy and powerful. A major revolution in the law thereby occurred, although it took about twenty years after adoption of the Federal Rules for the transformation to be felt in practice.

In the same period much of the American judiciary, led by the U.S. Supreme Court, was engaged in broad redefinition of the law. This period of judicial activism is epitomized in *Brown v. Board of Education* and the ensuing cases directly and indirectly related to desegregation—involving free speech, equality in voting, the right to legal assistance, and consumer rights. A similarly oriented activism was evident before *Brown* in such fields as personal injury law, privacy, legal accountability of government officials, free speech, and criminal justice. These changes more or less coincided with a great expansion of federal statutory law, defining legal relationships between individuals and business enterprises and between citizens and government. Examples include the Securities Acts of 1933 and 1934 (damage remedy for securities purchased on the basis of misleading promotion), the Fair Labor Standards Act of 1937 (damage remedies for employer violation of wage and hour regulations), the Voting Rights Act of 1965 (right to sue for unequal treatment of voters), the Equal Employment Acts of 1967–1991 (right to sue for race, gender, and age discrimination in employment), and various state consumer protection statutes (damages remedy for misleading sales promotions). Pervasive legislative policy, as well as judicial activism, has made civil litigation an instrument for asserting new legal rights. Civil litigation thus has become a primary mechanism by which private citizens and groups can enforce the law and resort to the courts to remake the law.

Changes in procedure and substantive law have been accompanied by a reaffirmation of the right of jury trial, particularly in the federal courts. Prior to 1938, the Supreme Court interpreted the right to jury trial to apply only to damages actions based on traditional common law.[1] Through a series of decisions in the period 1940–1980, the right of jury trial was extended to most damages actions based on new statutory rights and to many cases where injunctive relief was sought.[2] Most state courts also have given broad scope to jury trial, particularly in damages suits. The right to jury trial thus is available in most civil litigation except for domestic relations matters, administration of decedents' estates and bankruptcy proceedings.[3]

As will be discussed in the following section, important constraints remain on the use of civil litigation to secure legal rights. Furthermore, in the last decade or so bitter objections have been raised to the volume, cost, and intrusiveness of civil litigation. Various remedies have been proposed, such as limiting the scope of discovery. The Republican administrations from 1980 onward appointed judges who were conservative in their orientation to the law, in ordinary civil litigation as well as in criminal and constitutional law. However, this conservative tendency in the federal judiciary will not inevitably evolve into a long-term trend. The state courts, which handle the vast bulk of litigation, have not been strongly influenced by conservative sentiment. The principle of open discovery has wide popular appeal, particularly in a society that remains suspicious of secrecy on the part of government and business corporations. The right to jury trial is highly prized by both

populist and conservative sentiment. Congress and the state legislatures have declined to adopt changes in procedure that would
significantly alter the present balance of power between plaintiffs
and defendants. On the contrary, each new cycle of legislation has
tended to enlarge rather than constrict the legal remedies available
to the ordinary citizen against the government and business.

Critics rarely confront the scope of the legal changes that would
be necessary to alleviate the "curse of hyperlexis." Significant reduction of civil litigation and its costs would require such measures
as replacing tort liability in automobile cases with a no-fault system
providing limited compensation for injured victims; comprehensive
medical and income-replacement insurance for accident-caused injuries outside of the auto accident field; retrenching the scope of
antidiscrimination rights of suit covering race, gender, age, and
disability discrimination; similarly retrenching rights and remedies
in financial and commercial transactions, such as the securities laws;
creating rights of secrecy for business and government documents;
and relying on criminal law and regulatory systems to provide the
controls that presently are accomplished by civil liability. Most
critics of the present system prefer to complain about symptoms
rather than confront the political and social resistance that alternatives such as these will provoke. Hence, it is unlikely that the
present system will be significantly changed in the foreseeable future.

Constraints on Litigation

Although civil litigation is highly visible in the American
political scene, resort to litigation is in fact exceptional. In most
situations where the injured party has a legally provable claim, the
loss is covered by the victim's own insurance (for example, medical
insurance) or simply absorbed as a misfortune. Litigation ordinarily
is pursued only in cases of serious injury resulting from conduct
whose legal wrongfulness is at least reasonably arguable.

The primary constraint is cost, which from one viewpoint is

ironic. The aim of the Federal Rules is to reduce the cost of litigation by eliminating technicalities in pleading and permitting disclosure of all the relevant evidence. The underlying premise was that parties would make full disclosure of evidence promptly and voluntarily, and thereby eliminate "gaming" in litigation. More-or-less voluntary disclosure of evidence by both parties is indeed the practice in routine types of litigation, such as automobile accident cases and most divorce litigation.

However, the practice often is otherwise in litigation in which a plaintiff seeks to establish new rights or to uncover hidden wrongs, and in cases touching on issues of social or political justice. This type of litigation, whether involving business corporations or government bureaus, often threatens the defendant's economic, political, or legal viability. Rapid changes in substantive law in the last thirty years have overridden traditional practices in such fields as employee relations, financial transactions, police operations, and treatment of the environment. However, many business and government organizations have been slow to change their traditional practices in response and hence may be exposed to staggering losses when legal liability finally overtakes them. Notable examples of such legal catastrophes include those suffered by industries involved in the manufacture and use of asbestos products, the federal government in the case of the savings and loan industry crisis, and local government in various kinds of municipal activities. With such consequences at stake in a lawsuit, litigation readily becomes intense and protracted, and procedural issues often are the subject of major subsidiary litigation. Under these conditions, the quest for complete justice—among all the parties as to all the facts—can become self-defeating.

Also constraining civil justice as a social remedy are the rules concerning allocation of the costs of litigation. The American rule protects an unsuccessful plaintiff against having to pay defendant's attorneys. By the same token, however, the American rule precludes a successful plaintiff from recovering his attorneys' fees as well as the damages sustained. Hence, the plaintiff must be able to finance litigation from his or her own resources, or find a lawyer who will undertake the case on a contingent fee. Financing litigation from the plaintiff's own resources is generally possible only for businesses, wealthy individuals, and the government. Finding a lawyer who will proceed on a contingent fee is an option available only where the prospective recovery is large enough to warrant the lawyer's investment of time and effort. This ordinarily limits the prosecution of civil claims to those where liability is very clear and to those involving large damages. Moreover, the more complicated the case, the more difficult is the task of financing it.

Prospective defendants will defend litigation on a corresponding basis. Many defendants exposed to frequent claims adopt the strategy of vigorously defending every suit that is filed against them, counting on that policy to be a deterrent. Claimants who anticipate that their claims matter will be contested ordinarily will not go forward. Claims against defendants who cannot afford to put up a defense will result in default judgments. However, default judgments are often of little practical value because a defendant who is unable to pay a lawyer also will usually be unable to pay a judgment.

The iron law of economics in administration of justice is not unique to the American system. The hard fact that administering justice is costly explains why systems of administered justice have always been unjust to those who cannot afford to litigate. What is unique about the American system is its aspiration: to achieve finely calibrated justice covering an extensive array of rights enforceable through an expensive procedure that affords open discovery, jury trial, and liberal opportunity to seek redress in the appellate courts.

A related constraint on the effectiveness of civil justice arises from practical difficulties in the enforcement of judgments. Under American procedure the winning party, rather than the court, has primary responsibility for inducing the losing party to comply with the judgment. The remedy of injunction may be frustrated where the defendant lapses into inaction or is incapable of effective compliance. Claims against a defendant in financial distress often must be settled for a fraction of their value. Civil justice is most effective in dealing with claims for damages that are of substantial amount but not so large as to threaten the defendant's continued financial existence.

The use of civil justice as a mechanism of law reform is subject to important moral and political constraints as well. There is injustice in refusing to change the law in response to changed social conditions or emergent conceptions of social justice, but there is also injustice in imposing additional legal obligations after the fact.

Perhaps the greatest constraint on the resort to civil justice is the psychological distress that litigation inevitably involves. Learned Hand, one of our greatest judges, said, "As a litigant I should dread a lawsuit beyond almost anything else short of sickness and death."[4] A shared recognition of the ugliness of litigation may explain why most people hesitate to sue over legal grievances. Historical studies indicate that the volume of litigation in the present day is not radically greater than in earlier times. Studies of personal injury cases indicate that a high percentage of legally valid medical malpractice claims are not pursued; the same is very likely true of claims involving other wrongs, such as employment discrimination and breach of contract in business transactions. Thus, while Americans look to the courts to pronounce the norms for many relationships, only in extreme cases do they resort to actual enforcement. In this light, civil justice is as much a mechanism for community debate and civic instruction as for redressing legal wrongs. A society as culturally heterogenous and morally centered as ours may have a fundamental need for such a mechanism. If providing civic instruction is an undeclared function of the judiciary, then calculation of the costs and benefits of civil justice should take that benefit into account.

Continuities and Innovations

Despite the burdens that modern civil litigation imposes on the American courts, the system continues to function more or less effectively. Most cases are relatively simple and the vast majority of litigation is settled without trial. Each side retains a lawyer who investigates the facts by interviewing the client, examining documents provided by the client, inspecting public records (such as police reports in automobile accidents), and gathering information from third-party witnesses. Subsequent proceedings usually go no further than depositions of the parties and sometimes of key witnesses. Fewer than 5 percent of the cases will go to trial, and most trials will take only two or three days, and very few trials will be followed by an appeal. The whole process of such "ordinary litigation" plods along and yields results that leave the parties at peace and more or less satisfied that their claims and defenses were given consideration.

A small fraction of cases, however, looms large. These cases are weighty in one or more respects—large financial stakes, controversial political issues, litigants having high social visibility (such as political figures or movie stars), novel issues of law, many claimants (for example, victims of an airline crash or environmental pollution), or charges against several defendants who dispute among themselves as to their responsibility. This kind of litigation is a challenge to the system's capabilities, but also an opportunity to provide a measure of justice that a less versatile system could not accommodate. There is also a substantial amount of litigation that falls between the large volume of "ordinary" litigation and the small number of large cases that strain the capabilities of the system.

The problem for the system of civil justice is to accommodate this mixture of demands rationally and with reasonable efficiency. Various rules and methods of judicial administration have evolved. A basic principle of judicial administration is that different types of procedures should be provided for different types of cases. In the American system a rough classification of this kind is accomplished through the differentiation between the state and federal court systems. State courts handle most ordinary litigation and many of the cases of intermediate complexity, and only occasionally deal with large complex litigation. Federal courts have a large share of the complex cases and a relatively small portion of the ordinary litigation cases. However, because this allocation is imperfect, each system must deal with all three kinds of cases.

Within each court system, distinct administrative procedures are employed that reflect the system's case "portfolio." Thus, the procedure for considering pretrial motions in state court is designed on the assumption that the necessary rulings can be made quickly and without elaborate argument. Hence, such motions are handled very rapidly, with short legal briefs and allowing for oral argument only in exceptional situations. In contrast, the administrative procedures in federal court reflect the fact that pretrial motions in complex cases often involve legally complicated issues touching on jurisdiction, discovery, and preliminary issues concerning the merits. Motions in federal court therefore ordinarily will be given more extensive consideration. Moreover, in federal court a judge is assigned to preside in the case from start to finish; an assistant judge (a magistrate or a special referee) may assist in administering the pretrial stage; in cases involving large numbers of documents, a central documents repository may be established, with its own documents librarian. Special requirements may be imposed on discovery of expert and scientific evidence.

Other techniques seek to reduce acrimony in litigation, and thus its efficiency. Some courts have adopted "codes of civility" to reduce contentiousness, particularly in pretrial discovery. Other courts seek to enforce more rigorously the existing rules of procedural and professional ethics. Bar associations have sought to reinvigorate the sense of collegiality among advocates. These measures, if pursued on a sustained basis, can have beneficial effects in ameliorating the aversive characteristics of litigation. However, many lawyers tend to persist in "hard-ball" tactics. Effective judicial administration requires a high level of skill in interpersonal relationships, which many judges lack. A more fundamental obstacle is the reluctance of the political branches of government—the legislature and the executive—to provide the funds and the personnel needed by the courts for handling high volumes of litigation.

Behind the reluctance to commit political energy to improving the system is the hope that some new and somehow magical procedures can be devised for eliminating delays and inefficiencies in litigation. Changes that would make substantial differences would have to be radical in terms of substantive law or procedure or both, and no political consensus has emerged to support reform in such scope. Hence, procedural innovations in the last fifty years have been limited to relatively minor adjustments of the established procedural system. Viewed in this light, the effective administration of civil justice continues to be a never-ending task involving much drudgery, but nevertheless a necessary function of government in a civilized society. Perhaps the greatest obstacle to realizing improvement in the administration of justice is getting the various constituencies—judges, lawyers, litigants, and the public—to accept that simple fact.

Legal Justice and Social Justice

The American procedural system seeks to give expression to appealing political ideals. It may be helpful to examine those ideals more directly.

One ideal is equality of persons before the law. This ideal is exemplified in pleading rules that permit a statement of legal grievance in the language of the ordinary citizen, unburdened by esoteric legal terminology. Similarly, the liberal discovery rules aim to permit a plaintiff to obtain whatever evidence may support the grievance and a defendant to obtain whatever evidence may refute or mitigate liability. The rule permitting contingent fees aims to permit access to justice for a grievant who cannot afford to pay a lawyer. The right to jury trial invokes conceptions of justice in the community at large as well as principles of justice as understood by judges and lawyers.

Another ideal is autonomy of the individual. American procedural rules empower an aggrieved citizen to bring suit, to uncover evidence in the hands of an indifferent or hostile organization, and to submit the whole matter to a group of fellow citizens. Assistance in asserting such grievances is provided by a legal profession that is free to assert novel claims on the basis of a contingent fee or no fee at all. Individual legal grievances may be adopted by political or social action groups dedicated in matters such as consumer protection, free speech, due process, racial equality, and legal rights of women, children, the aged, the mentally disabled, property owners, stockholders, and taxpayers. Litigation in such cases may expand the rights of individuals and thereby their sense of autonomy.

A related ideal is freedom from the toils of bureaucratic government and business organizations. The system of civil litigation permits these regimes to be called to account before the law. The curative effect of such legal responsibility, it is hoped, will induce those who exercise authority to make amends for the past and to be more responsible in the future.

Another ideal is openness in transactions that affect important personal and social interests. Democratic politics is necessarily an open process. Just as the Constitution requires Congress to record its proceedings, and freedom of information statutes require disclosure of the business of the executive departments, so ready access to the courts, broad discovery, and jury trial make the quest for civil justice visible to the public at large.

The fundamental problem for American civil justice is to accommodate these ideals—equality, access, autonomy, and openness in civil justice—to the reality that their fulfillment entails economic, political, and moral costs. Making that accommodation poses essentially the same practical problems as popular aspirations for universal education, medical care, and economic security.

NOTES

Preface

1. Alexis de Tocqueville, *Democracy in America,* ed. J. P. Mayer and M. Lerner (New York: Harper and Row, 1966), 248.

2. *Brown v. Board of Education,* 347 U.S. 483 (1954).

3. *Roe v. Wade,* 410 U.S. 113 (1973).

CHAPTER 1: *History*

1. Humber Ferry Case, YB. Lib. Ass., pl. 41, f. 94; cited in S. Milsom, *Historical Foundations of the Common Law,* 2d ed. (London: Butterworths, 1981).

CHAPTER 2: *The Legal System and the Structure of Government*

1. U.S. Constitution, Art. VI, par. 2.

2. *Mullane v. Central Hanover Bank & Trust Co.,* 339 U.S. 306 (1950).

3. E.g., *City of Cleburne v. Cleburne Living Center,* 473 U.S. 432 (1985).

4. See Laurence H. Tribe, *American Constitutional Law,* 2d ed. (Mineola: Foundation Press, 1988).

5. U.S. Constitution, Art. IV, sec. 1.

6. *United States v. Nixon,* 418 U.S. 683 (1974).

7. California Constitution, Art. VI, sec. 1.

8. Rottman and Osterman, "Caseloads in the State Courts: Volume, Composition and Growth," 15 *State Court Journal* 4 (1991).

CHAPTER 3: *The Authority and Functions of American Courts*

1. *Marbury v. Madison,* 1 Cranch 137, 177 (U.S. 1803).

2. See Summers, "Statutory Interpretation in the United States," 407ff.

3. Robert Bork, a judge of the intermediate federal appellate court, was nominated by President Reagan to the Supreme Court, but was denied confirmation by the Senate after a bitter dispute about his suitability to be on the Court. Opponents conceded that he had high intellectual qualifications, but contended that he had a reactionary outlook and that he was unconcerned with the interests of women and minorities. Discussions from different viewpoints of the rejection of the nomination of Judge Bork include E. Bonner, *Battle for Justice* (New York: Norton, 1989) and P. McGuigan and D. Weyrich, *Ninth Justice: The Fight for Bork* (Washington: Free Congress Research and Education Foundation, 1990).

4. Attributed to Andrew Jackson as a response to *Worcester v. Georgia,* 31 U.S. 515 (6 Pet. 1832), by Horace Greeley in *The American Conflict: A History of the Great Rebellion* (Hartford: O. D. Case, 1864), 1: 106.

5. *Dred Scott v. Sandford,* 60 U.S. 393 (1856).

CHAPTER 4: *Concepts of Law and Legal Proof*

1. This analysis draws upon Michael Oakeshott, *On Human Conduct* (Oxford: Oxford University Press, 1975).

2. See R. Summers and M. Taruffo, "Interpretation and Comparative Analysis," in MacCormick and Summers, *Interpreting Statutes.*

3. See mainly M. Taruffo, *La motivazione della sentenza civile* (Padua: University of Padua, 1975), 112ff. and 207ff.

CHAPTER 6: *The Pretrial Stage*

1. H. Maine, *Dissertations on Early Law and Custom* (1883), 389.

2. *New York Times v. Sullivan,* 376 U.S. 254 (1964).

3. See MacCoun, Lind, and Tyler, "Alternative Dispute Resolution in Trial and Appellate Courts," in D. Kagehiro and W. Laufer, eds., *Handbook of Psychology and Law* (New York: Springer, 1992).

4. *Société Nationale Industrielle Aerospatiale v. United States District Court,* 482 U.S. 522 (1987).

CHAPTER 7: *The Trial*

1. *Beacon Theatres, Inc. v. Westover,* 359 U.S. 500, 510–511 (1959).
2. See *Granfinanciera, S.A. v. Nordberg,* 492 U.S. 33 (1989).

CHAPTER 11: *Perspectives of the American System*

1. *American Life Insurance v. Stewart,* 300 U.S. 203 (1937).
2. *Ross v. Bernhard,* 396 U.S. 531 (1970).
3. *Chauffeurs Union No. 391 v. Terry,* 494 U.S. 558 (1990).
4. Hand, "The Deficiencies of Trials to Reach the Heart of the Matter,"
3 *Ass'n Bar City of N.Y. Lectures on Legal Topics* 87 (1926).

BIBLIOGRAPHY

Citations pertaining to specific topics are listed by chapter after the general bibliography.

GENERAL

American Bar Association. *Standards of Judicial Administration*. Chicago: ABA, 1976.

Brilmayer, L. An Introduction to Jurisdiction in the American Federal System. Charlottesville: Michie, 1986.

Carrington, P., D. Meador, and M. Rosenberg. *Justice on Appeal*. St. Paul: West, 1976.

Chemerinsky, E. *Federal Jurisdiction*. Boston: Little, Brown, 1989.

Cleary, E., et al. *McCormick's Evidence*. 4th ed. St. Paul: West, 1992.

Dawson, J. *A History of Lay Judges*. Cambridge: Harvard University Press, 1960.

Devitt, E., C. Blackmar, and W. Wolf. *Federal Jury Instructions and Practice*. 4th ed. St. Paul: West, 1987.

Dobbs, D. *Remedies*. St. Paul: West, 1973.

Friedenthal, J., M. Kane, and A. Miller. *Civil Procedure*. St. Paul: West, 1985.

Friedman, L. *A History of American Law*. 2d ed. New York: Simon and Schuster, 1985.

Hazard, G., and J. Vetter. *Perspectives on Civil Procedure*. Boston: Little, Brown, 1987.

Holdsworth, W. *A History of English Law*. 7th ed. A. Goodhart and H. Hanbury, eds. London: Methuen, 1973.

James, F., G. Hazard, and J. Leubsdorf. *Civil Procedure*. 4th ed. Boston: Little, Brown, 1992.

Kalven, H., and H. Zeisel. *The American Jury*. Boston: Little, Brown, 1966.

Millar, R. *Civil Procedure of the Trial Court in Historical Perspective*. New York: National Conference of Judicial Councils, 1952.

Moore, J. *Moore's Federal Practice*. Albany: Matthew Bender, 1988.

Scoles, E., and P. Hay. *Conflict of Laws*. St. Paul: West, 1984.

Stern, R. *Appellate Practice in the United States*. 2d ed. Washington: BNA Books, 1988.

Wright, C. *Law of Federal Courts*. 4th ed. St. Paul: West, 1983.

Wright, C., A. Miller, and M. Kane. *Federal Practice and Procedure*. St. Paul: West, 1985.

Preface

James, Hazard, and Leubsdorf, *Civil Procedure*.

Hazard and Vetter. *Perspectives on Civil Procedure*.

Taruffo, M. "Diritto processuale civil nei paesi anglosassoni." In *Digesto delle discipline privatistiche*. Vol. 6, *Sezione civile*. Turin: UTET, 1990.

CHAPTER 1: *History*

Clark, C. *Code Pleading*. 2d ed. St. Paul: West, 1947.

Dawson, *History of Lay Judges*.

Friedman, *History of American Law*.

Holdsworth, *History of English Law*.

Millar, *Civil Procedure of the Trial Court*.

Milsom, S. *Historical Foundations of the Common Law*. 2d ed. London: Butterworths, 1981.

Wellington, H. *Interpreting the Constitution: The Supreme Court and the Process of Adjudication*. New Haven and London: Yale University Press, 1990.

CHAPTER 3: *The Authority and Functions of American Courts*

American Bar Association. *Judicial Selection, Tenure, and Compensation*. Chicago: ABA, 1971.

Ashman, A., and J. Alfini. *The Key to Judicial Merit Selection: The Nominating Process*. Chicago: American Judicature Society, 1974.

Bator, P., et al. *Hart & Wechsler's The Federal Courts and the Federal System.* 3d ed. Mineola: Foundation Press, 1988.

Chemerinsky, *Federal Jurisdiction.*

Grossman, J. *Lawyers and Judges: The American Bar Association and the Politics of Judicial Selection.* New York: Wiley, 1965.

LaFave, W., and J. Israel. *Criminal Procedure.* St. Paul: West, 1985.

Schwartz, B. *Administrative Law.* Boston: Little, Brown, 1991.

Stumpf, H., and J. Culve. *The Politics of State Courts.* White Plains, N.Y.: Longmans, 1992.

Summers, R. "Statutory Interpretation in the United States." In D. N. MacCormick and R. Summers, eds. *Interpreting Statutes: A Comparative Study.* Brookfield, Vt.: Dartmouth, 1991.

Summers, R., and M. Taruffo. "Interpretation and Comparative Analysis." In MacCormick and Summers, *Interpreting Statutes..*

Tribe, L. *American Constitutional Law.* 2d ed. Mineola: Foundation Press, 1988.

Wright, *Law of Federal Courts.*

CHAPTER 4: *Concepts of Law and Legal Proof*

Atiyah, P., and R. Summers. *Form and Substance in Anglo-American Law.* Oxford: Oxford University Press, 1987.

Austin, J. *Lectures in Jurisprudence.* 5th ed. G. Campbell, ed. London: John Murray, 1885.

Cleary et al. *McCormick's Evidence.*

Cohen, L. J. *The Probable and the Provable.* Oxford: Oxford University Press, 1977.

Damaška, M. *The Faces of Justice and State Authority: A Comparative Approach to the Legal Process.* New Haven and London: Yale University Press, 1986.

Dworkin, R. *Law's Empire.* Cambridge: Harvard University Press, 1986.

Hart, H. *The Concept of Law.* Oxford: Oxford University Press, 1961.

Hurst, W. *Law and Social Order in the United States.* Ithaca: Cornell University Press, 1977.

Kelsen, H. *General Theory of Law and State.* New York: Russell and Russell, 1961.

Levi, E. *An Introduction to Legal Reasoning.* Chicago: University of Chicago Press, 1963.

Reisman, M., and A. Schreiber. *Jurisprudence*. New Haven: New Haven Press, 1987.

Twining, W. *Rethinking Evidence: Exploratory Essays*. Oxford: Blackwell, 1990.

CHAPTER 5: *Lawyers and the Adversary System*

Cappelletti, M. *Public Interest Parties and the Active Role of the Judge in Civil Litigation*. Dobbs Ferry, N.Y.: Oceana, 1975.

Clermont and Eisenberg. "Trial by Jury or Judge? Transcending Empiricism." 77 *Cornell L. Rev.* 1124 (1992).

Dondi, A. *Introduzione della causa e strategie di difesa: Studi nelle scienze giuridiche e sociali*. Vol. 1, *Il modello statunitense*. Padua: University of Padua, 1991.

Frankel. "The Search for Truth: An Umperial View." 123 *U. Pa. L. Rev.* 1031 (1975).

Hazard, G. *Ethics in the Practice of Law*. New Haven and London: Yale University Press, 1978.

Hazard, G., and D. Rhode. *The Legal Profession: Responsibility and Regulation*. 2d ed. Mineola: Foundation Press, 1988.

Kaplan, von Mehren, and Schaefer. "Phases of German Procedure." 71 *Harv. L. Rev.* 1193, 1443 (1958).

Miller. "The Adversary System: Dinosaur or Phoenix?" 69 *Minn. L. Rev.* 1 (1984).

Taruffo, M. *Il processo civile "adversary" nell'esperienza americana*. Padua: University of Padua, 1979.

Thibaut, J., and L. Walker. *Procedural Justice: A Psychological Analysis*. Hillsdale, N.J.: L. Erlbaum Associates, 1975.

Underwood. "Adversary Ethics: More Dirty Tricks." 6 *Am. J. Trial Advoc.* 265 (1982).

Wolfram, C. *Modern Legal Ethics*. St. Paul: West, 1986.

CHAPTER 6: *The Pretrial Stage*

Dondi, A. *Effettività dei provvedimenti istruttori del giudice civile*. Padua: University of Padua, 1985.

Gottwald. "Simplified Civil Procedure in West Germany." 31 *Am. J. Comp. L.* 687 (1983).

Kaplan. "Reflections on the Comparison of Systems." 9 *Buff. L. Rev.* 409 (1960).

Langbein. "The German Advantage in Civil Procedure." 52 *U. Chi. L. Rev.* 823 (1985).

Pointer and Tigar. "Complex Litigation: Demonstration of Pretrial Conference." 6 *Rev. Litig.* 285 (1987).

Rosenberg, M. *The Pretrial Conference and Effective Justice.* New York: Columbia University Press, 1964.

Vairo. "Rule 11: A Critical Analysis." 118 *Federal Rules Decisions* 189 (1988).

CHAPTER 7: *The Trial*

Arnold. "A Historical Inquiry into the Right to Trial by Jury in Complex Civil Litigation." 128 *U. Pa. L. Rev.* 829 (1980).

Braithwaite, W. *Who Judges the Judges?* Chicago: American Bar Foundation, 1977.

Carrington. "The Seventh Amendment: Some Bicentennial Reflections." 1990 *U. Chi. Legal F.* 33.

Clermont and Eisenberg. "Trial by Jury or Judge?"

Comment. "Rethinking Limitations on the Peremptory Challenge." 85 *Colum. L. Rev.* 1357 (1985).

Gibson. "Jury Trials in Bankruptcy: Obeying the Commands of Article III and the Seventh Amendment." 72 *Minnesota L. Rev.* 967 (1988).

Kairys, Kadane, and Lehoczky. "Jury Representativeness: A Mandate for Multiple Source Lists." 65 *Cal. L. Rev.* 776 (1977).

Kalven, H., and H. Zeisel. *The American Jury.* Boston: Little, Brown, 1966.

Lempert. "Uncovering 'Nondiscernible' Differences: Empirical Research and the Jury-Size Cases." 73 *Mich. L. Rev.* 643 (1975).

Leubsdorf. "Theories of Judging and Judge Disqualification." 62 *N.Y.U. L. Rev.* 237 (1987).

Levitt, Nelson, Ball, and Chernick. "Expediting Voir Dire: An Empirical Study." 44 *S. Cal. L. Rev.* 916 (1971).

Note. "Article III Implications for the Applicability of the Seventh Amendment to Federal Statutory Actions." 95 *Yale L. J.* 1459 (1986).

Penrod, S., and D. Linz. "Voir Dire: Uses and Abuses." In M. F. Kaplan, ed. *The Impact of Social Psychology on Procedural Justice.* Springfield, Ill.: C. C. Thomas, 1986.

Schnapper. "Judges against Juries—Appellate Review of Federal Civil Jury Verdicts." 1989 *Wis. L. Rev.* 237.

Taruffo, M. *Studi sulla rilevanza della prova.* Padua: University of Padua, 1970.

Wolfram. "The Constitutional History of the Seventh Amendment." 57 *Minn. L. Rev.* 639 (1973).

Zeisel. "The Verdict of Five out of Six Civil Jurors: Constitutional Problems." 1982 *Am. B. Found. Res. J.* 141.

CHAPTER 8: *Procedural Variations*

Baird, D. *The Elements of Bankruptcy.* Mineola: Foundation Press, 1992.

Bell. "Serving Two Masters: Integration Ideals and Client Interests in School Desegregation Litigation." 85 *Yale L. J.* 470 (1976).

Clark, H. *Domestic Relations.* 2d ed. St. Paul: West, 1988.

Coffee. "Understanding the Plaintiff's Attorney: The Implications of Economic Theory for Private Enforcement of Law through Class and Derivative Actions." 86 *Colum. L. Rev.* 669 (1988).

Freer. "Rethinking Compulsory Joinder: A Proposal to Restructure Federal Rule 19." 60 *N.Y.U. L. Rev.* 1061 (1985).

Garth, Nagel, and Plager. "The Institution of the Private Attorney General: Perspectives from an Empirical Study of Class Action Litigation." 61 *S. Cal. L. Rev.* 353 (1988).

Goldberg, S., E. Green, and F. Sander. *Dispute Resolution.* Boston: Little, Brown, 1985.

Hazard and Moscovitz. "An Historical and Critical Analysis of Interpleader." 52 *Cal. L. Rev.* 706 (1964).

Lindblom, P., and G. Watson. *Courts and Lawyers Facing Complex Litigation Problems.* General report issued at the Eleventh World Conference on Procedural Law, Coimbra-Lisboa, Aug. 25–31, 1991.

MacCoun, Lind, and Tyler. "Alternative Dispute Resolution in Trial and Appellate Courts." In D. Kagehiro and W. Laufer, *Handbook of Psychology and Law.* New York: Springer, 1992.

Mullenix. "Class Resolution of the Mass-Tort Case: A Proposed Federal Procedure Act." 64 *Tex. L. Rev.* 1039 (1986).

Note. "Mandatory Mediation and Summary Jury Trial: Guidelines for Ensuring Fair and Effective Processes." 103 *Harv. L. Rev.* 1086 (1990).

Rhode. "Class Conflicts in Class Actions." 34 *Stan. L. Rev.* 1183 (1982).

Schoenbaum, T. *Admiralty and Maritime Law.* St. Paul: West, 1987.

Shapiro. "Some Thoughts on Intervention before Courts, Agencies, and Arbitrators." 81 *Harv. L. Rev.* 721 (1968).

Steele. "The Historical Context of Small Claims Courts." 1981 *Am. B. Found. Res. J.* 295.

Symposium. "Problems of Intervention in Public Law Litigation." 13 *U.C. Davis L. Rev.* 211 (1980).

Tobias. "Rule 19 and the Public Rights Exception to Party Joinder." 65 *N.C. L. Rev.* 745 (1987).

Yeazell. "From Group Litigation to Class Action." 27 *U.C.L.A. L. Rev.* 514 (1967).

CHAPTER 9: *Jurisdiction, Appeal, and Final Judgment*

American Bar Association. *Standards Relating to Appellate Courts.* Chicago: ABA, 1975.

Carrington, Meador, and Rosenberg. *Justice on Appeal.*

Karlen. "Civil Appeals: American and English Approaches Compared." 21 *Wm. & Mary L. Rev.* 121 (1979).

Martineau, R. *Modern Appellate Practice—Federal and State Civil Appeals.* Rochester, N.Y.: Lawyers Co-operative Publishing, 1983.

Pound, R. *Appellate Procedure in Civil Cases.* Boston: Little, Brown, 1941.

Restatement Second of Judgments. Philadelphia: American Law Institute, 1982.

Scoles, E., and P. Hay. *Conflict of Laws.* St. Paul: West, 1982.

Stern, R. *Appellate Practice in the United States.* Washington: Bureau of National Affairs, 1981.

Stern, R., and E. Gressman. *Supreme Court Practice.* 6th ed. Washington: Bureau of National Affairs, 1986.

Symposium. "Civil Appellate Jurisdiction.", 47 *Law & Contemp. Probs.* 1 (1984).

CHAPTER 10: *Enforcement of Judgments*

Dobbs, *Remedies*.

Laycock, D. The Death of the Irreparable Injury Rule. Oxford: Oxford University Press, 1991.

CHAPTER 11: *Perspectives of the American System*

Brazil, W. *Effective Approaches to Settlement: A Handbook for Lawyers and Judges*. Clifton, N.J.: Prentice-Hall Law and Business, 1988.

Brookings Institution. *Justice for All: Reducing Costs and Delay in Civil Litigation*. Washington: Brookings Institution, 1989.

Calamandrei, P. *Procedure and Democracy*. New York: New York University Press, 1956.

Cappelletti, M. *Access to Justice and the Welfare State*. Alphen aan den Rijn: Rijthoff, 1981.

Glendon, M. *Rights Talk: The Impoverishment of Political Discourse*. New York: Free Press, 1992.

Henderson and Munsterman. "Differentiated Case Management: A Report from the Field." 15 *State Court Journal* 25 (1991).

Hensler. "Trends in Tort Litigation: Findings from the Institute for Civil Justice's Research." 48 *Ohio St. L. J.* 479 (1987).

Janofsky. "The 'Big Case': A 'Big Burden' on Our Courts." 66 *A.B.A. J.* 848 (1990). Repr. in E. F. Hennessey, H. Clay, and T. B. Marvell, *Complex and Protracted Cases in State Courts*. Washington: Department of Justice, 1981.

O'Barr and Conley. "Lay Expectations of the Civil Justice System." 22 *Law and Society Review* 137 (1988).

State Court Caseload Statistics: Annual Report, 1988. Washington: Department of Justice, 1990.

Trubek. "The Costs of Ordinary Litigation." 31 *U.C.L.A. L. Rev.* 72 (1983).

INDEX